The GUINNESS Book of
Wild Flowers

Britain's Natural Heritage

The GUINNESS Book of

WILD
FLOWERS

Mary Briggs

Illustrations by Pamela Dowson

GUINNESS SUPERLATIVES LIMITED
2 CECIL COURT, LONDON ROAD, ENFIELD, MIDDLESEX

© Guideway Publishing Ltd 1980

Produced by Guideway Publishing Ltd

Published in 1980 by Guinness Superlatives Ltd,
2 Cecil Court, London Road, Enfield, Middlesex EN2 6DJ

Guinness is a registered trademark of
Guinness Superlatives Ltd

Briggs, Mary
The Guinness book of wild flowers.
(Britain's natural heritage).
1. Wild flowers - Great Britain
1. Title 11. Book of wild flowers 111. Series
582'. 13'0941 QK306
ISBN 0-85112-302-3

Printed by Morrison & Gibb Ltd, Edinburgh

The Publishers are grateful to the Botanical Society of the
British Isles for permission to use the distribution maps in
'Atlas of the British Flora' edited by Perring & Walker, as a
basis for the maps in this book; also to the BSBI for permission
to reproduce 'A Code of Conduct for the Conservation of Wild
Plants'.

To the Nature Conservancy Council for permission to
reproduce the list of National Nature Reserves.

The Publishers wish to thank the following for their permission
to reproduce photographs:

Front cover: (Marsh marigold) Heather Angel
Heather Angel: 51,53,55,57,59,61,63,65,67,69,71,73,75,
77,81,83,85,91,93,95,99,105,107,117,121,123,125,127,129,
131,135,137,139,143,145,147. S.F. Bisserot: 149. Mary Briggs:
97,113,115. W.F. Davidson: 87,103,111. Alan Outen: 119. John
Parkhurst: 79,89,101,109,141. S.M. Siems: 133.

Introduction

It is easy to take for granted the plant life around us. To many of us, vegetation does not have the immediate appeal or compelling interest of animals with their movement and sounds, or birds with song and soaring flight. However, plants in detail are full of interest and are rewarding to study; they are also of the greatest importance to man. Plants form the foundation of the chain of life; the ability of green plants to trap energy from sunlight, air and water is the basis on which all animal (including human) life on this earth ultimately depends. So the future of our plant life in Britain is of vital concern to all of us.

In the countryside we are at all times surrounded by plants, and it is different types of vegetation which form the changing colours and patterns of the landscape. Vegetation in turn is related to natural factors such as rocks, soils and climate; it is also very considerably influenced by man and, because of this, it is important that everyone should be aware of the impact made on the countryside by modern civilisation.

Historically, the activities of man have caused many changes in plant distribution: vast forests have been felled, partly for timber for the building of houses and ships and also for fuel and industry, and partly to clear more land for farming crops. These clearances changed the face of the land. In more recent times a dramatic alteration, especially in the south and east of England, has been the uprooting of some 4500 miles of hedgerows each year since 1945; this was done mainly to enlarge the fields growing crops, enabling farmers to use increasingly large cultivators and harvesting machines. Hedgerows provided shelter and some shade for a very varied range of plants, together with insects, birds and mammals, and the loss of so much of this specialised habitat, rich in species, has seriously affected our reserves of wildlife. Similarly the need for increased food production, necessary for our increased population, has led to much marginal land being transformed for agricultural use; with the clearance of odd corners and small strips of woodland such as the spinney, copse and rew (words more familiar to past generations), many habitats for wild plants have been lost.

Possibly the largest single factor affecting wild plants in Britain in recent times has been the drainage for agriculture and forestry of many acres of wetlands which formerly supported large and varied plant populations. Some of these species are now threatened with extinction. An example of this is the starfruit, *Damasonium alisma*, a water plant which grows in the shallow edges of muddy ponds. It has small ¼ in (6 mm), white, three-petalled flowers, which are followed by more conspicuous stalked heads of spiky green nutlets—giving the plant its name. The starfruit was once recorded as being present in 50 or more 10-kilometre squares in 13 counties from Hampshire to Yorkshire; by 1950 it had been reduced to only six squares and, since 1970, it has only been reliably reported from one locality, and is rapidly approaching extinction.

Another modern practice with widespread effects on plant life is the use of herbicides in cultivation to eliminate weeds. In particular many annual species have decreased dramatically, and seed production in these plants may be prevented for successive years. An example of this is the case of the pheasant's-eye, *Adonis annua*, an attractive small plant with scarlet, black-centred flowers and feathery green foliage. It was widespread through England as a casual plant in the early years of this century, but it can now be seen in only a handful of localities. Similarly the cornflower, *Centaurea cyanus*, was known throughout Britain in 1900, but in recent years it has rapidly become scarce and is now only occasionally seen in cornfields, mostly in Scotland.

Man's impact on vegetation can be traced through the centuries and back to prehistoric times. The seriousness of the present situation is due largely to the pressures of our rapidly increasing numbers; more land disappears under concrete and tarmac every day. Another important factor is the speed with which a habitat can be destroyed. Until this present century change was continuous, but at a slower pace and accompanied by continual adaptation by wildlife to the new conditions. Today, however, a habitat can disappear virtually overnight with the use of modern excavators and earth-moving equipment. Because of this, constant vigilance is necessary to safeguard threatened species.

Britain's flora has been very intensively studied, resulting in our knowledge that our wild flowers are extremely varied and, in some cases, very locally distributed. Although a great many of our native plants are decreasing in number, each one is important as part of the rich diversity. Each species also is part of an interlinked chain of life—for example, some insects are very specific and may depend on only one species of plant for food. Similarly, many plants are dependent on a particular insect for pollination, and some flowering plants, especially many orchids, are entirely dependent for germination on an association with a fungus species in the soil. This interdependence forms part of the chain of life and, with our knowledge of the many links still very incomplete, we break the chain at our own risk.

Contents

Identifying Wild Flowers

Wild flowers may be enjoyed in many ways. For some people the sight of those which are in sufficient numbers to bring colour to a country scene is a pleasure and possibly the only way in which they have seen wild flowers. By looking at individual flowers more closely, however, each one is found to be very different in detail and to have specific characteristics which are typical of that plant. The more we look at and for wild flowers, the more we find that our eyes focus on these details and pick out more than we have seen before. It is so easy to walk by small plants without even noticing them, but once we are on the look-out we can be sure of finding something of interest in any part of the countryside and of adding to our knowledge on a country walk at any season of the year.

Naming wild flowers can at first seem a daunting task—there are so many of them, 3000 in Britain alone. The flora of Britain is, in fact, relatively small because we are only on the fringe of a continent: areas such as that around the Mediterranean have larger floras with many more species. Britain's flora is outstandingly full of interest and it has been very intensively studied. It is one of the floras about which more is known, for the size of the area, than almost any other part of the world. Resulting from these studies, we have a very good selection of identification books for our flora, and in this we are fortunate. There are few parts of the world so well provided with this kind of literature—from that for beginners to the more advanced.

For the beginner, basic books may be divided in sections according to the colour of the flowers. This, with the size of the plant and the shape of the leaves, may give the first clues to the identification of the plant. From these a general name may be found for many wild flowers, but much more is learned about the flowers themselves by taking a closer look. The simpler books show only a selection of Britain's flowers; if one happens to be looking up one of those species included in the book, it is possible to name it—but there may well be many other similar plants not mentioned. For these a more comprehensive book is required. There are several good identification books which, without using many technical terms, include most of the plants one is likely to find in Britain. There is a bibliography at the end of this section for guidance.

To begin with, it is usually the pictures which are looked at first but all plants are variable. Each will change in appearance through all the stages of its life cycle, from young seedlings to the drying plants often with ripe fruits. It is not possible to show all these stages in a single illustration, and therefore a text with more information is essential.

For more specific identification it will be necessary to know the parts of the flower. The diagram of a flower in this section shows the main parts of a buttercup flower. This flower is regular in shape, with radial symmetry and is open with the main parts visible, i.e. it is a simple insect-pollinated flower. There are many variations in flower shape: in some the petals are fused and elongated into tubes; some are irregular in shape and enclose the central flower parts. However stamens (male parts) and gynoecium (female parts) are mostly present in all flowers. Most flowers have both male and female parts in the same flower; these are called hermaphrodites. On some plants there are

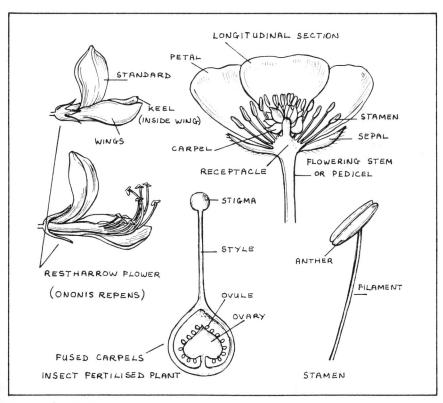

Topography of a flower

separate male and female flowers; these are monoecious or unisexual. And in some plants male flowers and female flowers are on separate plants; these are dioecious or bisexual.

One kind of hermaphrodite flower, but one which is irregular in shape, is a flower of the Papilionaceae, or pea, family (see page 11). In this flower a large upper petal forms an upright 'standard', the side petals come forward as wings and the two lower petals are fused to a boat-shaped keel. Familiar examples of this are the wild sweet peas, the larger-flowered sweet peas cultivated in our gardens and the smaller similar white flowers that appear on the vegetable.

Each stamen is made up of a stalk, or filament, and the anther containing the pollen grains. The stamens differ a great deal in shape, size and in their attachment to the inside of the flowers. The bog asphodel (see 'A Selection of Species') has conspicuously 'woolly' filaments to the stamens. These are an adaptation to damp habitats, particularly to wet weather when no insects are on the wing. The space between the group of stamens is filled with those long woolly hairs which trap and hold a droplet of water. Pollen grains shed from the anthers just above this float on the surface of the water droplet and, by this means, reach the stigma in the centre of the flower, in order that fertilisation can take place.

The gynoecium (female parts) is shown in the diagram in simple form: fused carpels, each containing a simple ovule with style and stigma. The stigma is receptive to the pollen grains. The sepals and petals are modified leaves. The main function of the sepals is to enclose and protect the flower buds, as the parts of the flower are often contained, fully formed, inside the bud for a long time—even in some plants for months—before the flowers open, and must be protected from inclement weather, particularly from rain. Petals are usually brightly coloured with the primary function of attracting insects to those flowers dependent on them for pollination. The veining on the petals is often directed towards glistening nectaries, attracting insects towards the sugary nectar—the insects will transfer the pollen from the anthers *en route* to their nectar feast. These markings are known as honey guides

The petals and stamens may be set above or below the ovary, a differentiation in form which gives a major division in the classification of the flowers. As more flowers are recognised, it becomes interesting to learn their classification into families—the plants of each family have the same basic characteristics in flower structure.

Some plants with hermaphrodite flowers have different

arrangements inside the flowers. A very good example of this is in primrose flowers. These are of two kinds, as shown in the diagram. The 'pin-eyed' flowers have the stamens low in the tube and a long style with the stigma at the top of the flowers. The 'thrum-eyed' flowers are the exact reverse in arrangement—the stigma on its short style is well down the tube, while the anthers in these flowers have long filaments to the top of the tube where the anthers cluster in line with the petal lobes. The word 'thrum' is a term used for the cut ends of wool in weaving, and is very descriptive of the buff-coloured tuft of stamens showing at the centre of the flower, quite distinct from those flowers centred by a rounded pale green, 'pin-eyed' stigma. This ingenious adaptation ensures cross-pollination between different plants (of great value for maintaining strong healthy stock in plants), as insects alighting on a 'pin-eyed' flower leave pollen from the stamens of a recently visited 'thrum-eyed' flower, and take pollen in the reverse direction as well.

In very recent years, it has been possible to examine these flower parts with electron microscopes and, with the very high magnifications, it can be seen that the stigmas of these types of flowers, although seeming the same to the naked eye, except for length of style, do in fact have a different surface structure so that pollen from 'thrum' plants will be held on the stigma of a 'pin' plant, while a 'pin' plant's own pollen will not fit into its own surface pattern. There is also a chemical attraction-and-rejection process involved, so that the whole procedure is in fact very much more complex than is at first apparent.

Other significant characteristics to look for are the different shapes of the leaves; our diagram shows some examples. The shapes and structure of fruits are also of prime importance, and can in themselves make a fascinating study.

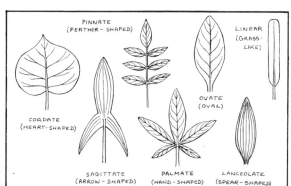

Leaf shapes

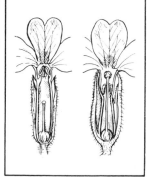

Cross section of a primrose

This leads us to perhaps the most important point of all in plant identification—this is the importance of *detail*. If you want to become familiar with the range of wild plants in our countryside, it is essential to have patience and a feeling for accuracy, as precise identification is going to take time and application. Of course, it is not necessary to take up detailed study to appreciate wild flowers, and many country lovers can enjoy them without knowing the names of them, or can restrict their enquiries to only the most common flowers. For those who choose to pursue a more detailed study, however, it can be a most rewarding hobby, providing a lifetime's interest and continual fascination.

As detail is of such essential importance, so for those studying wild flowers and the amateur botanist the most essential of equipment is a hand lens. This small magnifier, used to enlarge the smaller plants or parts of larger plants, opens up a new world of form and colour. Many small details may be barely noticeable with the eyes alone, or even impossible to see without magnification, but by using a hand lens these are brought into new focus and are often most beautiful. For example, the scarlet pimpernel flowers (see 'A Selection of Species'), when seen from the distance of our height above the ground, appear as tiny orange-scarlet flowers among green leaves, but, when seen through a lens, one discovers that each flower petal is fringed with tiny glandular hairs, and that the green stems and leaves are dotted with black glands. Very many tiny flowers are incredibly transformed when seen through a magnifying glass of a small hand lens. It is not only for enjoyment that a hand lens is essential; the details seen with the lens may often be the vital information necessary for the correct identification of the plant.

For precise identification a standard book called a 'Flora' is also necessary. In a Flora there will be comparative measurements enabling us to distinguish between closely related species. Another feature of a Flora is often identification 'keys': these are aids to naming, set out in the form of a series of alternative pairs of questions based on the diagnostic characteristics of the plant. These keys are very helpful as they highlight the most important characteristics for the identification of a species. They do use technical terms, but there will usually be a glossary explaining these included in the Flora.

One of the puzzling points in plant identification is that the distinction between species varies a great deal, in some cases because of very small details, e.g. two plants may be separated by one having hairs differently arranged on parts of the plant, or the shape of the fruit may differ between two species. In other cases, the variation within a single species may be so large—e.g. in size, flower-colour or hairiness—that two plants quite different in appearance may in fact be both identified as belonging to the same species. Here the botanical Flora can help to assess the differences shown by particular specimens. Some plant identification books print in italics the most important characteristics which differentiate similiar species. There can also be a certain 'jizz' (a term used by naturalists to describe their firm impression of a living thing's general appearance) to a growing plant—a combination of shape, texture and way of growth—but only from experience can we know the jizz of a plant.

Even those with the experience of a lifetime find that it is all too easy to be wrong occasionally—but it is perhaps this challenge which is so stimulating to a field botanist. For some particular species of plants there may be key features which stand out in the growing plant. For example, the round-leaved sundew flowers (see 'A Selection of Species') are shortlived and not too easily spotted on the thread-like flower stalks, but the sundew plants can be recognised during most of the year by the very characteristic red leaves glistening with sticky 'droplet' hairs. Similarly the bog asphodel, whose yellow flowers are upstanding and showy, also has conspicuous orange-red fruit capsules held upright on firm stalks which, for several weeks in the autumn, colour the damp flushes and mossy bogs where this plant grows.

The habitat where the plant grows also gives clues to the identity of the plants. Some such as herb robert (see 'A Selection of Species') can be found in widespread situations through the countryside, but many other wild flowers show a very specific adaptation to one particular habitat. This is seen, for example, in many of the flowers growing along the coast. The sea-kale (see 'A Selection of Species') is very specialised to resist the effects of salt which would cause normal tissues to shrink and wither. Even the globular fruits of the sea-kale are impervious to sea water and have air-filled cells which give the fruits buoyancy—they can float in the sea for several days without losing viability, and they are, therefore, often dispersed to grow in a suitable new locality further along the shore line by floating in the sea.

Another important point to notice is the flowering time—in most wild plants this occurs at a very specific time of the year. In spite of variation in the seasons—there may be a late spring so that all the spring-flowering plants will bloom late in that year—they still flower in the same sequence with the earliest spring-flowering plants opening first. With some groups of plants this can be a very positive aid to identification. For example, with the umbellifer plants (many of which are very similar in superficial appearance) there is a sequence of flowering times through the summer so that as the flowers of one species are going over to fruits, so another comes into full flower. Noticing this pattern of flowering in your area can be of considerable help in sorting out this difficult plant family.

The opening of flowers is dependent on many factors, including enzyme reactions within the plant, the air temperature and the length of daylight hours. As the days lengthen in spring, the bud-opening response in many plants is triggered off. Sometimes we find spring plants, such as violets and primroses, in flower in the autumn when the shortening days give the same number of daylight hours as the corresponding lengthening days of early spring.

Equipped now with a suitable identification book (or books) and a hand lens, there is still another important point to remember—that plants as living, changing subjects do vary at times from the typical. The descriptions in the identification books will refer to the average specimens, and in most cases the plants will fit the descriptions. However, many factors can affect the growth of plants: growing in an unusual habitat, on different soil, on a manure heap, at a different season, in unusual weather conditions, sprayed with herbicides, etc. In all these cases any particular species of plant may grow either 'starved' and be very miniature, or 'giant' and grow up to two or three times its normal size. Plants that have been touched by just a trace of herbicide spray may be very curiously coloured or distorted. Galls, caused by insect parasites or a virus, may also distort a leaf, flower or fruit to make it almost unrecognisable. There is also the possibility of hybrids between species, and numbers of varieties may give a plant an appearance not described in the books. All this would suggest that naming the wild flowers is indeed a difficult task, but these are the unusual plants, and most of those we do find fall into the range of typical characters. However there will always be some for which a certain identification is not easy, perhaps not even possible.

One of the puzzling aspects of plant identification is perhaps the initial definition of a species. This is based on the decisions made by taxonomists after long studies of each species of plant through its range of growth throughout the world. The Latin name currently given to a plant is, by international convention, the name used when that plant was first described. To find this first description often requires long historical research through botanical writings in different parts of the world. Sometimes an earlier name is unexpectedly discovered and the Latin name must then be changed to the earlier one given to that plant.

Another reason for changing the name may also be when botanists study the characters of a group of plants and find that, when they extend their studies of these plants to specimens from different countries or from different habitats, some previously named as different species may be the same plant, or vice versa. These changes of name may often be confusing to the field botanist. The Latin name of a familiar plant which has been known for generations is changed and the plant given a new name, testing the memories of those hoping to remember them. However, name changes are the inevitable consequence of new studies of plants and a further increase in our knowledge of the plant world. The Latin names used in this book are from *The Flora of the British Isles,* by Clapham, Tutin and Warburg, 2nd edition, 1962.

Most of our wild flowers have one or more country names in English, not so tongue-twisting as the Latin names. These names are of great interest in themselves, often reflecting the way of life from past generations. They often show great accuracy of observation and are an indication that the wild flowers were well known to our ancestors who used these names. Many of our wild flowers were given very many different names, often differing in each region of Britain and some of them are very local names. They are delightfully described by Geoffrey Grigson in his book *The Englishman's Flora.*

The country names often, too, indicate the uses and associations of the plants in former times. In the days when most people lived in or near the country, the plants around them were of great importance: many were used as food to supplement their diets, which were less varied than ours today with our imports from around the world. Our ancestors also turned to wild flowers for cures in times of sickness; many of these plants would have been effective, and some are still in use in medicine today. They are available as herbal medicines, but must be treated with caution when using them for self-medication, as many contain poisonous as well as beneficial compounds. The concentration of the chemical constituents of a plant may vary a great deal through the season, because of the age of the plant or through changes in the weather during the growth of the plant—standardisation of the medicinal properties is, therefore, a skilled practice. Plants should never be taken without great care and positively accurate identification.

For identification, these attractive local names are not always satisfactory as the same name was at times given to different plants, and often one plant was known by different names in different parts of the country. Today, to avoid confusion, we have a standard list of English names for wild flowers in Britain—the names and spellings in this book are taken from this list *(English Names of Wild Flowers,* by Dony, Rob and Perring, 1974)—but at the same time we hope not to lose entirely the country names with their links with past life-styles.

One fact which soon emerges in taking up an interest in plants is that it is not only an absorbing and fascinating study, but also an open-ended one. Naming all the plants of the countryside can be just the beginning and may lead to many rewarding further studies.

Books of Interest

For the very young

All about Poppies and Bluebells and Things (National Trust).

For the young

British Wild Flowers (Ladybird); *Hedges* (Ladybird); Humphries, *Spotter's Book of Wild Flowers* (Usborne); *I-Spy Wild Flowers*; *Plants and How They Grow* (Ladybird); *What to Look for in: Spring, Summer, Autumn, Winter*—4 books (Ladybird).

Field Identification Guides

Clapham, Tutin and Warburg, *The Excursion Flora of the British Isles,* 3rd edition (Cambridge University Press); *Field Guide in Colour to Wild Flowers* (Octopus); Fitter, Fitter and Blamey, *The Wild Flowers of Britain and Northern Europe* (Collins); Hubbard, *Grasses* (Pelican); Hyde and Wade, *Welsh Ferns* (National Museum of Cardiff); Jermy and Tutin, *British Sedges* (Botanical Society of the British Isles); Keble Martin, *The Concise British Flora in Colour* (Michael Joseph); McClintock and Fitter, *The Pocket Guide to Wild Flowers* (Collins); Nilsson and Mossberg, *Northern Orchids* (Penguin); Rose, *The Wild Flower Key to the British Isles* (Warne).

Reference Books

Bowen, *Introduction to Botany* (Newnes); Clapham, Tutin and Warburg, *Flora of the British Isles,* 2nd edition (Cambridge University Press); Dony, Rob, and Perring, *English Names of Wild Flowers* (Butterworth press); Holm and Bredsdorff, *The Biology of Flowers* (Penguin); Pervical, *Flora Biology* (Permagon); Perring and Farrell, *British Red data Book; Volume I, Vascular Plants* (Society for the Promotion of nature Conservancy); Perring and Walters *Atlas of the British Flora,* 2nd edition (Ep Publishing); Tansley and Proctor, *Britain's Green Mantle,* 2nd edition (Allen & Unwin).

Keeping Records

Keeping records of plants that we have seen can be very useful and interesting; records from the past have been invaluable in the changing conditions of the present. Achievements in the conservation of our wild flowers have depended upon the availability of reliable records of plant distribution—these are necessary to determine which of our plants are most threatened.

The earliest recording of plants in Britain dates back to the sixteenth century when William Turner, the physician and cleric who has been called 'The Father of British Botany', published two small books which contain the earliest printed records of British native plants. He later went on to write a larger work, *A New Herball*. Other British botanists followed. Thomas Johnson recorded, in his book, *Iter in Agrum Cantianum*, the journey through Kent of a party of ten botanists in 1629, listing the plants that they found on their way. In 1660 John Ray published his *Catalogus Plantarium circa Cantabrigiam*—a catalogue of the plants around Cambridge which was the first account of the flora of a single county in Britain. As Ray became more absorbed in his interest in botany, he travelled extensively around Britain and, in 1670 and 1690, he again published catalogues of British plants, classifying them in sections, many of which correspond to our present-day plant families.

Later, many good local plant lists and Floras were published from many parts of Britain. In 1932, G.C. Druce published *The Comital Flora of the British Isles* which covers the subject in a single volume—the first to deal with plant distribution through Great Britain, Ireland and the Channel Islands. In Druce's work, lists of counties in which the plants could be found are given plant by plant, and, by reference back to these lists, counties from which the plants had since become extinct could be ascertained.

In the 1950s a new printing process made it possible for plant records to be printed in the form of dot maps, each dot representing the presence of the plant in that particular area. This challenge was taken up by the members of the Botanical Society of the British Isles, who undertook a survey of the wild plants throughout Britain during the following ten years. The survey was based on the National Grid, using the ten-kilometre grid squares as the unit for the information of the presence or absence of each British plant. Recorders went to every ten-kilometre square in Britain, recording on field cards which had been specially printed for the survey, of which part of one is shown here. These listed abbreviations of the Latin names for the plants, some 949 on each card, and the recorder drew a line through the name of every plant seen. There was space for additional plants at the end of the card. These field cards, one for each ten-kilometre square, were, when edited, fed into the machine which printed a dot on the map of Britain in every square in which the plant had been recorded. The resulting maps were published as the *Atlas of the Flora of the British Isles* in 1962.

This survey, which has since been further updated, has been invaluable as a source of information on decreasing plant populations. From the maps, 300 species were selected as becoming rare and detailed studies on these species further highlighted those plants which are most seriously threatened. The results of these studies were published in 1977 as *The British Red Data Book I: Vascular Plants*. Since the completion of the plant atlas, many other groups have been similarly surveyed, including birds, reptiles, mammals and many groups of insects. Surveys on more than 50 groups are at present in hand, and distribution atlases have been published for birds, ferns, mosses, butterflies, snails and many others.

Recording as described above is a scientific tool for use in conservation in particular and in increasing our knowledge in general. But simpler, more personal records can also be of value, and are often very rewarding. Lists of plants from defined areas can be most useful for reference. Members of the Wild Flower Society have a large green diary containing the Latin names, in alphabetical order, of 1000 wild flowers, with spaces to enter where and when each flower is seen. Filling in this diary can also be recommended as a splendid way to learn the Latin names (so difficult for the beginner).

Plant lists can also be supplemented by drawings or photographs. By drawing a plant, its characteristics are often more accurately observed and memorised. It is usually unnecessarily wasteful to make collections of specimens, but there are some exceptions to this. Where plants are plentiful in a locality, to take a small specimen characteristic of the plant can be very helpful for study and for learning the special features of the plant for future identification. This is particularly useful for difficult groups of plants such as grasses and sedges. Most museums have herbaria with many dried specimens available for study on request. When deciding to collect specimens, keep in mind the rules and the law governing this. Learn carefully the 'Code of Conduct for the Conservation of Wild Plants' which is printed at the end of this book.

Photography is a very rewarding way of recording plants, yet even this must be undertaken with care, as it is all too easy to trample, kneel or even lie on other surrounding plants, most especially on small seedlings, when concentrating on one plant or flower. With the advent of colour films, flower photography has become very popular, and it was first thought that it would be a splendid safeguard to wild flowers—to photograph and not to pick seemed to be ideal—until it was realised that, especially where people congregate in numbers, photographer's feet can sometimes do enormous damage through trampling a fragile habitat. A recent report from the warden guarding one of our rarest and most threatened orchids told of two photographers who, without realising at all, lay happily on two small seedlings while they respectfully photographed another plant in flower—leaving the seedlings sadly crushed beyond recovery.

Wild flower photographers who keep these hazards in mind and carefully watch where they tread, lie or kneel can have an absorbing hobby. With so many plants to discover, there is plenty of scope for many years, and each year will bring unexpected delights to those looking for special pictures with a photographer's eye. On any wild plant walk there is the chance of finding one at its perfection of flowering, with perhaps a perfect group of flowers growing in the background. On the other hand, to take good photographs of many plants can take years—to find the ideal setting in good weather with a long-wanted plant just in flower can be a small triumph, and one of the many delights of being a plant hunter.

Grid Ref.	LOCALITY			SOUTH WEST	
				Date	V.C. No.
	HABITAT			V.C.	
				Alt.	Code No.

3	Acer	cam	177	Arum	neg	341	Carex acuti	520	Cirsi	pal	721	Equis tel	935	Glyce	ped

Wildflower record card

Britain's Flora through the Ages

The history of the vegetation of Britain is closely linked to the great climatic changes of past eras. In geological times before the Ice Ages, parts of Britain are known to have had tropical and sub-tropical climates. This is shown by fossil remains found at Bembridge on the Isle of Wight, the Isle of Sheppey and at Herne Bay, and in the London clay at Aldwick near Bognor in Sussex. Parts of tropical plants, such as the fruits of the nypa palm, have been found in these London clay deposits; today the nypa palm grows in brackish water along river estuaries in South-east Asia. Many other tropical plants with fossil remains in Britain are similar to those growing now in the Malayan islands; other fossil plants include magnolias, which grow in warm, temperate climates. It is thought that the plants of lowland Britain in that era would have resembled those now growing in the mountains of western China, in Japan, Burma and the Himalayas. Fossil-leaf remains from the Isle of Mull and other plant fossils found in Derbyshire and East Anglia show similar evidence of an early tropical climate and tropical plants in Britain.

An all-important event in the sequence of climatic changes followed this tropical and sub-tropical climate when a series of Ice Ages occurred during which Britain was almost completely covered by a great sheet of ice about 250 000 years ago. North of a line from the Thames to the Severn, the land lay crushed under the weight of this ice, nearly 3000 feet (1000 metres) thick in places, with only the highest mountain peaks appearing above it. As these ice sheets receded and advanced, U-shaped valleys were carved out of the highlands: these can still be seen today in the scenery typical of north Wales, the Scottish Highlands and the Lake District.

At the edge of the ice, only a few arctic animals, such as the mammoth, musk ox and woolly rhinoceros, could survive the freezing temperatures and inhospitable conditions, and a few hardy plant species, mainly lichens and mosses, took up residence in this bleak landscape. During these thousands of years of the ice cap retreating and again advancing, plants colonised the land as the ice melted so that the vegetation fluctuated from heathland to forest then to arctic flora.

On mountain crags above the ice, plants which could tolerate subarctic conditions at high altitudes were able to survive. In Upper

Teesdale today, an arctic-alpine plant community can still be seen, growing there as an isolated pocket of vegetation from the times of the Ice Ages through the thousands of years until the present day. The spring gentian (*Gentiana verna*), thrift (*Armeria maritima*)—see 'A Selection of Species' for both of these — and other rare mountain plants in this area are known as 'relict' plants—from the flora before the ice. Similar arctic plants can be found in the high corries of Snowdonia in Wales and in the Scottish Highlands.

The Teesdale plants are of particular interest to botanists because of the continuity of that plant community—it is not known just how they survived, but evidence shows that today's plants are very similar to those growing in late glacial times. When much of Britain was later covered by forest, the Teesdale uplands remained as short turf, leaving the plants there as a record of the vegetation which must have covered most of Britain until the end of the Ice Ages—a unique and irreplaceable scientific record. Because of this, in 1967 botanists fought a bill through Parliament in an attempt to save the area from being drowned under the reservoir at Cow Green proposed by I.C.I. —a conservation battle which, although it was not won, has since been acclaimed as a milestone in conservation history. For the first time attention was drawn to the importance of plants, and plants

The Great Ice Age

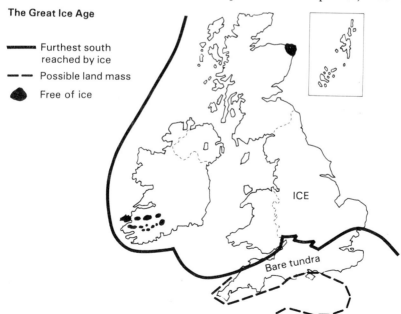

Furthest south
reached by ice

Possible land mass

Free of ice

ICE

Bare tundra

were shown to be worthy of a fight. Because the unique nature of this site was highlighted, I.C.I. donated a large fund for research into the area, enabling the parts of the site to be affected by the reservoir to be fully recorded and documented before immersion.

In the 1930s the new technique of pollen analysis of peats and sediments was introduced into Britain by Professor Harry Godwin at Cambridge. By boring deep into peat deposits and taking a core, samples of soil many thousands of years old can be examined. Similar core samples can be taken from the sediment under muddy lakes. Peat is accumulated decayed plant remains formed in waterlogged, and often acid, situations; under these conditions bacterial decay is very slow and it is possible to identify some plant remains in the peat. Pollen grains and spores in particular are suitable for this type of examination because of their impervious coating. The chemical nature of this outer coat makes them extremely resistant to the micro-organisms of decay: there is no anaerobic micro-organism (those not requiring oxygen) which can cause the decay of the outer coat of spores and pollen grains. Because of this, spore from ferns, horsetails and some mosses and nearly all pollen grains survive; these can be readily identified by the use of modern high-powered microscopes and, as each is characteristic of its plant family and sometimes even of a particular species, the plants which were growing on the land at the time when the peat was laid down can now be known. The dates of the successive layers of peat can be determined very accurately by another recent modern technique—carbon dating. This is a method of dating material from once-living compounds at least 100 years old up to 20 000 years or even older. This dating is based on the structure of a form of a carbon atom known as C_{14} which is radioactive. This radioactivity is slowly lost at a fixed rate—by measuring the residual radiation, the age can be calculated; in other words, the lower the radiation, the greater the age.

From the study of the pollen grains found in successive layers of peat, it has been possible to show, through carbon dating, that after the Ice Ages in Britain, from about 10 000 BC much of our land was covered by tundra—a low arctic heath, frozen for much of the year but supporting small plants and shrubs. These were mostly lichens and mosses, but also small arctic flowering plants and berry-bearing shrubs such as the bilberry (*Vaccinium myrtillus*) and other related shrubs, and also a few stunted creeping willows and birches, but no upright trees. Tundra still covers large areas in Scandinavia, Canada and the Arctic Soviet Union.

As temperature rose, the tundra was rapidly replaced by

grassland, followed by trees—juniper, birch and pine, with alder (a tree of swamps and streamsides) in wet places. Trees then greatly increased in number and much of the land was finally covered by mixed oak forest. The remainder of the land, where it was unsuitable for trees, was covered by blanket peat bogs. At this time Britain was still part of mainland Europe, joined by a land-bridge to the Continent when the sea-level was lower. The date of Britain's final separation from the continental mainland is not precisely known but is thought to have occurred about 5500 BC. Some time earlier Ireland had been separated from Great Britain. Once the British Isles were all surrounded by sea, the climate modified into the Atlantic climate and the vegetation gradually evolved into the familiar plants of the countryside today.

Climate is still a vital factor in plant distribution today—the mountain pansy (*Viola lutea*— see 'A Selection of Species'), for example, occurs in almost every county in north-west Britain, north and west of a line from the Humber to the Severn. In all these localities can be found upland areas where the summers are cool and the rainfall high—conditions ideally suited to the little mountain pansy. This is an alpine plant found throughout the continental alpine range—in contrast to those of our mountain plants which are arctic in origin and to

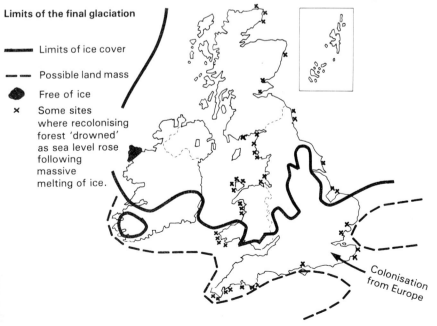

Limits of the final glaciation

——— Limits of ice cover

— — Possible land mass

Free of ice

× Some sites where recolonising forest 'drowned' as sea level rose following massive melting of ice.

Colonisation from Europe

be found also in Scandinavia. The rather patchy and local distribution of the mountain pansy is related also to its specific soil preferences.

There is a surprising discrepancy between Britain's flora and many of the plants which grow just across the English Channel. This may be due to the forest vegetation of Britain just before the sea swept over the land-bridge joining the mainland. Some of the plants which grow on the French side of the Channel are intolerant of shade so would not have survived under the forest trees of Britain. Later these forests were cleared by man but, by then, the sea was an effective barrier to any plant migration. On the other hand, southern England does support some plants which also live on the Continent, including some which are frost-sensitive but can survive on the south coast. An example of this is the rare relative of the Italian lords-and-ladies, *Arum italicum* (very similar in appearance to the lords-and-ladies which is featured in this book), which, in this country, grows only in an area in which snow lies, on average, for less than five days in the year.

The changes through climate and weathering are a continual process, and we can ourselves observe the effects. An example is when we find heather *Calluna vulgaris* (see 'A Selection of Species'), a plant which is completely intolerant of lime in the soil, growing on the chalk downs. These pockets of heather growing with acid-loving plants are found on the high ridges of downland where rain has leached the calcium out of the soil in the form of organic acids. This leaves a neutral soil in which heather can flourish, usually surrounded by the typical downland flowers of chalk vegetation on the encircling slopes.

Studies in Britain's past vegetation continue and more information on the plants of the past comes to light every year. The knowledge of the flora of Britain as it is today compares well with that known of any country in the world, but this knowledge is still incomplete—new plants are still being found. Since 1950 three species new to Britain have been discovered in remote areas of Scotland: Lapland diapensia *(Diapensia lapponica)*, Norwegian mugwort *(Artemisia norvegica)* and Iceland-purslane *(Koenigia islandica)*. It is not surprising, therefore, that, in spite of the detailed information on the flora in Britain of the last 10 000 years now building up through the study of pollen grains and spores, there are still many gaps in our knowledge of the plants which grew in Britain in past ages.

World-wide Distribution of Plants

The distribution of plants around the world can be traced back to prehistory when the continents were joined, more or less, into one land mass surrounded by sea. At one time it was thought that flowering plants might have evolved only after the continents had drifted apart, but recent research has shown evidence of some flowering plants moving with the continental drift. The present distribution of some closely-related species can only be explained by the land movements proposed by geological theories.

As the land masses were shifting and breaking, some islands became isolated, separated by miles of ocean. Plants on these islands developed along individual lines, sometimes parallel to the development of mainland plants, but always distinctive as island flora. In Britain, our flora does have certain island characteristics, and many of our smaller offshore islands also have their own specialised and distinctive floras.

Throughout the world, plants with a profusion of rainbow-coloured, richly-scented flowers show an almost unbelievable diversity of shape, colour and form. These different shapes and colours have evolved very largely as adaptations for pollination and, in many cases, in association with insect pollinators particular to that part of the world. Extreme examples of these are orchids with the curious flowers which mimic the insects in pattern and colour, but also in texture—often the lip petal is 'furry' with soft hairs—and, in some types, it even has a similar scent. In this way the pollinating insect is attracted to the flower. Many other flowers are also, but less obviously, adapted. In hedgerows, wild honeysuckle with long tubular spurs holding nectar at their base are visited by moths and butterflies with very long tongues—nectar-reaching when uncoiled.

Of the 250 000 species of flowering plants in the world, most of the families are tropical in their distribution, and sadly this very rich tropical flora is now extremely threatened. As more land is needed for growing more food as populations increase, and for urbanisation and for highways, and more timber is required for modern man's insatiable need for paper and building, so the forests are felled at an alarming rate. Unesco has issued figures estimating that 2.5 million acres (10 million hectares) of tropical forest are being felled each year—equal to the area of the Royal Botanic Gardens at Kew being destroyed approximately every 6½ minutes. At this rate of destruction there may well be no tropical forests left in the world by the end of this century. Many flower species may disappear before they have been described or classified, and many with possible uses as medicine or for food may well be extinct before there has been time to make any detailed studies or evaluation.

Continental drift

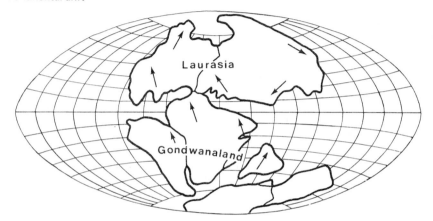

180 million years ago

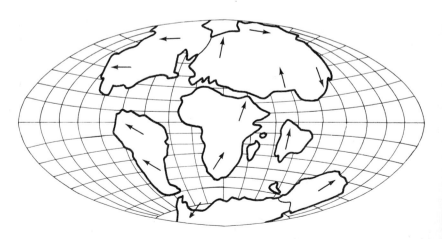

65 million years ago

Introduced Species

In the earlier chapter on the history of British vegetation we noted that Britain was separated from the continental mainland at some time around 5500 BC. Since Britain has been surrounded by sea, plants have been unable to spread into this country by natural dispersal. There are a few very isolated examples of still viable seeds being swept on to our shores from across the sea, and there is the possibility that some plants might be carried over on the feet or plumage of birds. In general, however, natural plant dispersal by land from the Continent will have ceased by the time the English Channel was formed, and the flora of the early post-glacial period (after 5500 BC) can be regarded as the true native flora of Britain. Since then, the hundreds of new additions to our wild plants have almost all been introduced by man, either deliberately or accidentally.

Before the arrival of neolithic man (about 3000 BC), the natural vegetation of Britain was forest. From pollen analysis studies, it can be shown that once man was on the scene the number of forest trees gradually declined as neolithic man was able to fell large trees with his polished stone axes, made from flints and rocks, to open up clearings in the forest for his settlements and for growing crops. Thus, in neolithic times, man was capable of destroying extensive areas of forest which was, in time, replaced by grasslands and heaths. When agriculture was primitive, the forest clearings would soon revert to scrub and then again to forest as the nomadic men moved on.

However, by 400 BC, farming practices among the Celtic people were more advanced, and with the arrival of the Romans there are written records of corn exports and imports to Britain. Cornfield weeds became the first wild flowers recorded as introductions by man. (A weed has been defined as a wild flower growing where it is not wanted by man.) The cultivation method which turns over soil leaving it bare as was done in these early cornfields offers an ideal habitat for plant colonisers, especially the annual species. Cornfield weeds introduced by the Romans include many which have been familiar in Britain's fields from then until very recently: common poppy (*Papaver rhoeas*—see 'A Selection of Species'), the scarlet pheasant's-eye (*Adonis annua*), the cornflower (*Centaurea cyanus*)—lending its name to the lovely shade 'cornflower blue'—and the corncockle (*Agrostemma githago*), with its pale rose-purple petals and long, spreading, star-like sepal teeth.

These plants have all been part of our landscape for many centuries. Only in the past 30 years have they become less common through the use of herbicides and, especially in the case of cornfield weeds, the screening to produce clean seed for farm crops. Until the end of the last century, corn seed was winnowed by hand in a current of air to separate it from the chaff and some of the lighter weed seeds. When threshing machinery came into use, a steady, continous air current increased winnowing efficiency, and the smaller weed seeds were separated by a fine mesh which held back the grains of corn and larger seeds while allowing small seeds to drop through.

A flower whose seeds measure less than ⅛ inch (2.8 mm)—the size of the mesh—and which was formerly widespread growing in cornfields is thorow-wax (*Bupleurum rotundifolium*). This greyish-green, rather waxy plant has oval or roundish leaves which surround the stem, giving the impression of the leaves being threaded on the stem. 'Wax' is an old English word meaning 'grow', and William Turner in *The Names of Herbes* (1548) wrote : 'It may be called in englishe Thorowax, because the stalke waxeth throwe the leaves.' The heads of its tiny yellow flowers are also surrounded by rounded green bracts. It was formerly recorded from nearly 50 counties in England but, in 1960, it was known in only four counties and is now considered to be extinct in Britain.

The spread of many wild plants has been along the transport routes of man through the ages. Many of the flowers that occurred alongside the paths and trackways of early times have country names associated with these, for example, traveller's joy (*Clematis vitalba*—see 'A Selection of Species'), and 'waybread', an old name for the greater plantain (*Plantago major*), a plant which can withstand much trampling. When the Roman soldiers arrived and built their famous roads across the country north to Hadrian's Wall, the spread of wild flower seeds was rapid. Roman roads had sloping embankments, giving many miles of open ground ideal for the colonisation of plants. Added to this was the heavy traffic movement helpful to the dispersal of seeds, and the many loads of imported grain for feeding the legions of soldiers would have certainly contained many seeds of the cornfield flowers from the southern areas where the corn had been harvested. Among the plants first recorded from Britain in the Roman era, most probably introduced on Roman sandals or on their chariot wheels, are scarlet pimpernel (*Anagallis arvensis*—see 'A Selection of Species') and the colourful corn marigold (*Chrysanthemum segetum*).

Scarlet pimpernel

In more recent times the construction of the railways provided similar habitats for colonising plants. An example of this is Oxford ragwort (*Senecio squalidus*), first grown in this country in the Oxford Botanic Garden as a specimen plant from Sicily. Like other ragworts, its seeds have small parachutes of silky hairs and they are wind dispersed. Outside the Botanic Garden, it was first seen growing on walls in Oxford, but when railway lines crossed the country the plant spread rapidly along the embankments and today is widespread through England. Railway embankments were famous for their displays of wild flowers. In more leisurely times the banks were scythed by hand—today labour-saving herbicide control destroys most of the colourful flowers of past years. Following recent closures of many lines, some disused railways have now been taken over as nature reserves, and the embankments are once again managed, not only for wild flowers but also for insects, birds and wild animals.

Indian balsam

Another 'highway' along which plants can travel to colonise new ground is by water. Plants can colonise the banks, as does Indian balsam (*Impatiens glandulifera*). This native of the Himalayas is a tall, robust, handsome plant growing to six feet (1.8 m) with large flowers ranging in colour from purple through pinks to white. It was first introduced as a garden plant in 1839, but in this century it has colonised along the banks of most of our rivers. When its seeds are ripe the fruit capsules burst open explosively, throwing the seeds some distance from the parent plant. At the waterside this proves to be a very efficient dispersal system as some seeds will be carried down the river to colonise a new stretch of riverbank. Similarly, other balsams have gained a foothold in Britain, including the orange balsam (*Impatiens capensis*), also known as a jewel weed, which came from eastern North America and is now spreading along rivers and canals in southern Britain.

Other plants using waterways are aquatics spreading through the water itself. The Canadian waterweed (*Elodea canadensis*) was introduced early in the nineteenth century and spread very rapidly along canals to ponds and ditches, often in great abundance. Almost all its flowers produced in Britain are female, and fertile seeds have not been recorded—the phenomenal spread of this plant was entirely vegetative, fragments of broken plants in the water growing into new plants, and each year more new plants growing from the overwintering 'winter buds'.

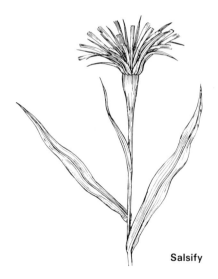

Salsify

Another group of introduced plants is that which was imported for food and grown in herb gardens and kitchen gardens. Some have since escaped and become naturalised in the countryside. An example is salsify (*Tragopogon porrifolius*), introduced from the Mediterranean countries and grown for its long taproot which is eaten as a vegetable. Similar in shape to our native yellow-flowered goat's beard (*Tragopogon pratensis*), the salsify has flowers which are dull purple.

'Jack-go-to-bed-at-noon' is a country name which describes the very consistent habit of this family of plants whose flowers open in the early morning light and close around midday.

A plant naturalised from herb gardens is (*Angelica archangelica*). Larger than our native wild angelica (*Angelica sylvestris*) it is this 'archangelica' which is grown for its succulent green stems which are crystallised and used as the strips of green in cake decoration. This large umbellifer plant has become naturalised in a few places and along the River Thames near Kew Gardens.

Oxford ragwort, mentioned earlier, grows in its native Sicily on soils of volcanic ash from Mount Etna. During the last war, this flower was one of the first and most vigorous found colonising the ash and rubble of London bomb sites. Another colourful plant which colonised and grew massed in the bomb sites of London and other cities was the rosebay willowherb (*Chamaenerion angustifolium*). Sometimes also called 'fireweed' from its habit of colonising after fires, this plant, with its large rose-purple spikes of flowers, is one that is known to have grown in Britain in late-glacial times, but in this century it was restricted to mountain and some woodland habitats until wartime bombing provided new open sites suitable for colonisation. This is a plant with an exceptionally efficient wind-dispersal system for its seeds: again each carries a parachute of long silky hairs and about 70 of these swell and contract at the base according to the humidity of the atmosphere, so that the parachute will close in damp weather and spread out when the air is dry, to ensure wide dispersal. Added to this is its prodigious seed production—each seed pod contains up to 500 seeds so that *one* average plant may produce 80 000 seeds. It is no wonder that, in a suitable habitat, colonisation by this plant can be very rapid and efficient.

Another plant introduced into Britain following a war was the hoary cress (*Cardaria draba*), a native of central and southern Europe and western Asia. First recorded in this country in 1809, this plant is said to have been introduced after the ill-fated battle on the island of Walcheren in the Napoleonic War. The soldiers, stricken with fever, were brought to Ramsgate on palliases stuffed with hay which were later given to a Thanet farmer who ploughed the hay into his fields as manure. The cress then appeared in great quantity, spreading across the Isle of Thanet in following years; one of its English names is still Thanet cress as a reminder of this historic introduction. Today this plant has spread in great abundance along the south coast of England—growing primarily on coastal shingles and waste places.

Hoary cress

Again on the south coast but this time in one locality only, is the starry clover (*Trifolium stellatum*) which is naturalised at Shoreham Harbour in Sussex where it was first recorded in 1804. This small clover has conspicuously star-shaped fruiting heads with softly silky, starry sepal teeth. Presumably some of these were brought into harbour on a cargo ship—possibly from Greece or the Mediterranean islands—and the plant became established on the shingle around the harbour. Despite increased building through the years—the shingle has now almost completely disappeared under bungalows—each year one or two starry clover plants can still be found persisting in some odd corner near the beach. In the countries around the Mediterranean, this clover is a very common wayside plant, but it is not frost-resistent so has not spread further north in Britain.

Starry clover

Some of the plants which have been introduced into gardens have 'escaped' to become naturalised features of the countryside well away from cultivation. An example of this is the Japanese knotweed *(Polygonum cuspidatum)*. From Japan as its name suggests, it is a large erect perennial growing to 5 feet (1.5 metres) with broad alternate leaves on stems which are sometimes curved at the tip, and terminal spikes of small creamy flowers. This plant can be invasive, and large clumps are often seen by roadsides or growing in waste places.

Another plant which is spreading from gardens is, in contrast to the last, a very tiny creeping plant. The slender speedwell (*Veronica filiformis*), from Asia Minor and the Caucasus, is similar to germander speedwell (featured in this book) but with smaller, rounder leaves and paler blue flowers. This was first introduced to Britain early in the last century, but in about 1920 it became fashionable as a rock plant, and from the rockery it spread very invasively through gardens. Like Canadian waterweed it is not known to have fertile seed in this country, but, as it roots very freely from the nodes (where the leaves join the stem), each tiny fragment of this brittle plant falling on a scrap of soil can grow into a new spreading plant. It has been suggested that in the lean years of post-war depression lawn mowers were not owned by many people and lending the lawn mower was a custom of the times. Fragments of slender speedwell could have been passed from garden to garden attached to the wheels of the mower. Certainly today if one takes a train journey to Brighton in April, from the raised rail embankment you can see that the lawns in the gardens below are sheets of blue as this speedwell has replaced the grass. Away from gardens this pretty plant (but tiresome garden weed) is spreading along river banks and farm tracks.

A completely alien group of plants has come into Britain in the sheep wool imported from Australia and New Zealand. The waste wool from the cleaned fleeces is known as 'shoddy' and this is sold to farmers for manuring light soils. On farms where shoddy has been spread on the fields, or on waste shoddy dumps, many strange plants from the Southern Hemisphere can be found—often flowering in late autumn (their springtime) until the first frosts kill them off. These 'shoddy' plants can give an exciting and colourful display of wild flowers previously unknown in Britain.

Other sources of strange plants come from the bird seed sold to feed caged birds - some of the seed is swept out with the cage cleanings, carried to the municipal rubbish dump where they may germinate to be found by those field botanists who are rubbish dump enthusiasts. An example of these plants is one which looks similar to the previously mentioned thorow-wax (also called 'hare's-ear'), is frequently mistaken for it and has appeared as a recent introduction through bird seed fed to caged birds or wild birds in the garden. This is the related long-leaved hare's-ear (*Bupleurum lancifolium*), which is found from time to time near gardens and on rubbish tips. It is common in southern Europe. Those seeds which escape being eaten will germinate and flower, but in Britain this plant does not persist as it is not sufficiently hardy to withstand our winter temperatures.

Other exotic plants may be found outside spice mills where seeds of plants strange and puzzling to us in Britain may grow occasionally. Many plant seeds have hooks or bristles which catch on to human clothing or animal fur and may be transported many miles by this means.

New plants appear all the time. In 1979 there were three records of a lobelia from California which had not been seen as a wild plant in Britain before. Each of the sightings of this small plant with blue-and-white flowers similar in shape to the garden lobelia was made by the edge of a newly-constructed lake or reservoir. On investigation it was found that a grass seed mix from America had been sown to stabilise the soil at the water's edge—the seed of the lobelia flower (*Downingia elegans*), a wayside plant in California, must have been in with the grass seed.

The spontaneous appearance of a new, strange wild plant can be very exciting and some enthusiasts enjoy making a special study of these. Most new arrivals do not persist, but occasionally an introduced plant can find a suitable habitat—the correct ecological niche for that plant—and then it may flourish, spread and establish itself to become part of Britain's flora.

Conservation:
An Historical Introduction

Although there was, until very recently, an implicit belief that the natural world was inexhaustible, there have been, since the early years of this century, a handful of far-sighted pioneers who have seen the signs of decrease in the quantity or, in some cases, in the number of species of plants.

One such pioneer was Nathaniel Charles Rothschild (1877-1923), who was promoting conservation at the turn of the century. He was well ahead of his time in realising that not only individual species must be watched and saved if threatened with extinction, but that it was even more important to protect and conserve habitats of different ecological patterns. With his clear-sighted penetration of future conditions he saw, too, the importance of gaining public support through widespread publicity, and that it would be crucial to gain Government support for conservation efforts. With these considerations in mind he launched his Society for the Promotion of Nature Reserves (SPNR) in 1912 (now the Society for the Promotion of Nature Conservation). Lord Rothschild not only left a generous legacy to this new society, but he also donated part of Wicken Fen to the National Trust. It was indeed a significant gift. This example of the fenland, which once covered large areas of East Anglia and provided a way of life for those who lived there, is now largely drained, giving great scientific and heritage value to the remaining areas of fen. Sadly, Rothchild's provisional plan to acquire further reserves was seriously set back by the First World War, followed soon after by his own illness and early death.

Another pioneer was Sir Maurice Abbot-Anderson who wrote in 1928, in the book *Our Vanishing Wild Flowers,* an 'afterword to all those who have the preservation and protection of wild flowers at heart', in which he set out the aims and rules of Flora's League. This society was promoted by the Council for the Protection of Rural England. Members received a badge and a small pamphlet incorporating the following rules:

Don't pick wild flowers, *cut* them; picking disturbs the roots.

Don't *dig up* plants; they seldom grow when transplanted.

Don't pick *early* in the day; they only wither.

Don't pick *many*; leave for others to enjoy as well.

He added that 'wild flowers, once picked, soon wither, and then give joy to no one, not even the picker; whereas if left to bloom, they are admired in their own surroundings by all who have eyes to see'. With the excellent intention of getting this message to young people, flower posters for colouring were distributed free to schools, but lack of funds finally curtailed the activities of Flora's League.

It was not until the Second World War that the nature conservation movement strengthened. In particular, a new list of areas to be investigated was drawn up so that those of the highest scientific value could be given priority for conservation. At this time attention was directed particularly to salt-marshes, shingle beaches and to marshlands in the Midlands (known as 'mosses'), as all these were recognised as characteristic types of wild country in England having no exact counterpart in continental Europe.

In 1949 the Nature Conservancy was established as the official Government body for representation of nature conservation to the State. By 1977 this body (later called the Nature Conservancy Council) had declared 161 National Nature Reserves in Britain—51 091 acres (126 246 hectares) in total.

At the time of the establishment of the Nature Conservancy, the voluntary movements were beginning to play a large role in the provision of local reserves across the country. Since the Second World War the SPNR has focused attention on the formation of County Trusts for Nature Conservation throughout Britain, until, by 1979, there was a Trust in every county with a membership of 120 000. Between them they own about 1 200 reserves, and it is estimated that a new reserve is acquired by the Trusts at the approximate rate of one or two per week.

Also during the post-war years, the Botanical Society of the British Isles (BSBI) appointed a committee to investigate reported threats to our rare plants and to take swift action when necessary. Many sites were saved, but some also were lost, sometimes because knowledge of the rarity was not communicated in time. Now that a site can disappear almost overnight with the use of modern earth-moving equipment and other large machines, it has become increasingly important that all varieties should be documented. It was also realised that, before formulating a plan to protect our plants, it was essential to have accurate knowledge of present distributions. The BSBI launched a national survey in which members recorded every 10-kilometre square of the National Grid, listing all the wild plants in each. The results were published in the *Atlas of the British Flora* in 1962. From these maps it could be seen at a glance which plants were most threatened and that some were in danger of extinction.

As a result of this research, it was agreed that legislation for the protection of plants was necessary. For many years the Wild Plant Protection Working Party, comprising members of BSBI, SPNR and the Council for Nature, worked on a bill to put to Parliament. After several set-backs, finally the Wild Creatures and Wild Plants Conservation Act, 1975 became the law of the land. It is now an offence in Britain to uproot any wild plant without the permission of the landowner, or to pick, uproot or destroy any of the 21 (in 1975) protected plants.

Societies and Nature Reserves

Societies

In Britain we have a long tradition of amateur naturalists which is unique. The number and variety of societies we can join is very large. Through past years the careful recording by these many amateurs has greatly contributed to our knowledge of British wild flowers.

The Botanical Society of the British Isles

Founded in 1836, the leading botanical society in Britain is an association of amateur and professional botanists whose common interest lies in the study of British flowering plants and ferns. The society publishes the journal *Watsonia, BSBI Abstracts* and *BSBI News,* all covering a wide range of topics relating to British plants, and also publishes local Floras, handbooks and conference reports. It arranges conferences, exhibitions and field meetings. Members can get help with identification of difficult plants. Part of the society's concern is with conservation: local and countrywide surveys (in which members take part) are organised; the society has sponsored legislation for wild plants, and has widely circulated conservation leaflets and posters. For more information, contact: B.S.B.I., c/o Department of Botany, British Museum (Natural History), Cromwell Road, London SW7 5BD.

The Botanical Society of Edinburgh

This national society in Scotland arranges lecture and field meetings for the study of wild plants in Scotland. Some meetings are held jointly with the B.S.B.I. (see above). Publications include *Proceeddings* and *B.S.E. News.* For further information, contact: The Secretary, B.S.E., Botany Department, University of Edinburgh, Mayfield Road, Edinburgh EH9 3JH.

British Trust for Conservation Volunteers
For those who would like to join in practical work for conservation, such as land management, contact: B.T.C.V., c/o Zoological Society of London, Regent's Park, London NW1 4RY.

Council for the Protection of Rural England
Concerned for the countryside of England, the C.P.R.E. sponsored the pioneer plant-protection society, 'Flora's League'. Leaflets published include 'Wild Flower Sense' and 'Hedgerows'. For further information contact: C.P.R.E., 4 Hobart Place, London SW1W OHY.

Council for the Protection of Rural Wales
This is the Welsh counterpart to the C.P.R.E. and its aim and concern are the same but related to Wales. For more information, contact: C.P.R.W.,14 Broad Street, Welshpool, Powys SY21 7SD.

County Trusts for Nature Conservation
See Society for the Promotion of Nature Conservation.

Field Studies Council
The F.S.C. owns ten centres in different parts of England and Wales, where residential courses are available on a variety of natural history subjects, including wild flowers. Attendance at these is an excellent way to learn more about wild plants in Britain, and amateur naturalists are especially welcomed. For further information,contact: F.S.C., 9 Devereux Court, Strand, London WC2R 3JR.

In Scotland, there is the **Scottish Field Studies Association**, whose residential courses are held mainly at Kindrogan Field Centre, Blairgowrie, Perthshire, with some courses also at Lamlash, Isle of Arran. These cover all aspects of the countryside, including mountain wild flowers. Again, amateurs are welcome. For more information, contact: S.F.S.A. Ltd, 158 Craigcrook Road, Edinburgh EH4 3PP.

Local Natural History Societies

For information on the ones in your area, apply to your local public library.

The National Trust for Places of Historic Interest or Natural Beauty

The National Trust—perhaps more widely known for its ownership and maintenance of stately homes and historic buildings—has also made a major contribution to the conservation of wildlife habitats. Considered by the Trust to be its 'most priceless asset' is the wealth of open spaces which include wild hill country of the Lake District, Snowdonia, the Scottish Highlands and the Brecon Beacons, fenland in East Anglia, a lough in Ireland, woods, islands and southern downland. All who are concerned for and enjoy Britain's countryside must be grateful that so many acres of outstanding beauty and interest are held permanently by the Trust for all and for future generations.

Some 350 of the thousands of Trust properties are listed by the Nature Conservancy Council as SSSIs (Sites of Special Scientific Interest); many of these are maintained for special botanical interest. Britain's coastline is an irreplaceable part of our island's heritage; many miles have been acquired through 'Enterprise Neptune'—a scheme launched in 1965 in response to increasing threats to this vulnerable habitat. The National Trust now owns and safeguards more than 400 miles of Britain's varied coastline.

Many walks have been set up on Trust land and naturalists can find an abundance of wild flowers, with other features of interest—all the areas are marked with the familiar Trust 'oak leaf' sign. It is forbidden to pick flowers on National Trust properties—these flowers must be left for all to enjoy.

For further information and a leaflet contact: The National Trust, 42 Queen Anne's Gate, London SW1H 9AS. There is also a National Trust for Scotland contact: 5 Charlotte Square, Edinburgh EH2 4DU.

The Scottish Wildlife Trust

The national body concerned with all forms of wildlife in Scotland owns 35 nature reserves of which six are open to the public. For more information, contact: S.W.T., 8 Dublin Street, Edinburgh EH1 3PP.

Society for the Promotion of Nature Conservation

This 'umbrella' society coordinates voluntary conservation work in all the County Trusts for Nature Conservation. There is a Trust in every county in England and Wales, owning between them 1200 nature reserves. The Society will be able to tell you where the County Trust is nearest you.

The S.P.N.C. also has a junior branch called **WATCH,** which organises projects and competitions for 8 to 15 year olds.

For information on the S.P.N.C., WATCH and local county Trusts, contact: The Green, Nettleham, Lincoln LN2 2NR.

Ulster Trust for Nature Conservation

Those living in Northern Ireland who are interested in the conservation of wildlife of that area should contact: U.T.N.C., c/o I. Forsyth, Esq., Department of Extra-Mural Studies, The Queen's University, Belfast BE7 INN.

The Wild Flower Society

This is a friendly society for enthusiasts. Members have a plant diary for entries of wild flowers found, and there are local branch secretaries who advise on identifications. A magazine is published three times a year and field meetings are arranged. For more information, contact: W.F.S., 62 London Road, Reading, Berkshire RG1 5AS.

The World Wildlife Fund (British National Appeal)

This society donates funds to projects concerned with the protection of Britain's wild plants, among other campaigns. Grants are given towards research projects for conservation, for wardening sites, and for publication of leaflets for education and to spread the conservation message—as well as for the purchase of special reserves. For further information, contact: W.W.F., 29 Greville Street, London EC1N 8AX.

Nature Reserves

In many parts of Britain the country scene is changing rapidly through the pressures of modern times and similarly throughout the world as human populations increase. To some extent plants can adapt to changing conditions and some wild flowers survive surprisingly well in urbanised surroundings at times—giving continual opportunities to look for plants of interest. However, careful watch on decreasing plants is necessary to guard the most vulnerable and most seriously threatened species, and in particular to ensure that suitable habitats are saved for all the different types of wild flowers. Not only the rarest of our wild flowers need protection such as this, but some which we think of as still growing abundantly may show sudden and rapid decrease in numbers. An example is the bluebell, one of Britain's most typical plants: even today's teenagers tell us that many of the woods full of bluebells which they remember from their younger days have already vanished. Against this eventuality, some of our most treasured plants are saved now in reserves. A map and list of Britain's reserves and wildfowl refuges are included in this book.

When a site is declared a nature reserve, that in itself does not mean the end of problems—careful and continuous management is necessary to maintain suitable growing conditions for the plant or plants to be protected. Most sites which just have a 'keep out' fence around them soon become overgrown; the less aggressive plants, are then unable to compete against invading scrub or coarser vegetation. Some form of grazing or clearance by hand is often necessary and the Britaish Trust for Conservation Volunteers (see above) can call on groups of volunteers for reserve management tasks. On the other hand, on a site left open and unprotected, special plants may be damaged accidentally, or even occasionally by deliberate vandalism.

In 1979, a colony of 60 especially fine bee orchids, recorded as part of a research project, were uprooted from a site by some unscrupulous and selfish thief.

One of the difficult decisions on reserves which have rare flowers is public access. It is realised that people like to see rare plants growing in their natural habitat, but many trampling feet in a small restricted area can be fatally destructive, crushing the surrounding vegetation and compacting the soil so that young plants and seedlings may be inadvertently destroyed. For example, in the Upper Teesdale National Nature Reserve, the plants are small and vulnerable and it is very important to keep to the paths that are the public rights of way.

In some instances arrangements have been made at a reserve to allow a very special wild flower to be seen with no damage to the plants of the habitat. Examples of these are at the Rex Graham Reserve for the military orchid and the Framsden fritillary field. Both are in Suffolk and are owned by the Suffolk Trust for Nature Conservation, which organises an open day each year at each reserve when the orchids and the fritillaries are in flower—but these reserves are firmly closed for the rest of the year for undisturbed plant growth. Special paths have been constructed and boarding laid down to enable large numbers of people to see these beautiful flowers without damage to the sites. Further details, and dates of open day at each reserve, from: Suffolk Trust for Nature Conservaton, St Peter's House, Cutler Street, Ipswich, Suffolk. This Trust in Suffolk may be pioneering the way for the future—possibly this may be the *only* way we shall be able to see some of our rarest plants in years ahead.

Many other reserves are open to the public, although in some cases a permit to visit may be required. There are, however, a few reserves in which the habitat is already fragile and these may be particularly susceptible to trampling feet—the balance for survival is already delicately poised in these few cases and visits here must be restricted to only very limited access for study or research. We can all help to protect our rarities by respecting requests not to visit (as these are made only when essential in the particular circumstances) and by following the 'Code of Conduct for the Conservation of Wild Plants' (included in this book) at all times.

The Nature Conservancy Council is the official government body which promotes nature conservation in Britain, and advises the Government and all those whose activities affect our wildlife and wild places. The Conservancy also selects, establishes and manages a series of National Nature Reserves (a map and listing of these are included in this book). The main purpose for these reserves is the protection and conservation of habitats and rare species of wildlife—including plants—and for scientific research to increase our knowledge of our environment and our ability to conserve in the future.

In addition, there are a further 50 or so local nature reserves which have been established and are managed by local authorities around Britain. For information on local reserves apply to the planning department of the local county or regional council. The Forestry Commission also has large areas set aside for wildlife conservation on the Commission's lands. Many fine forest walks and nature trails have been laid out for public use; information about these is available from: The Forestry Commission, 231 Corstorphine Road, Edinburgh EH12 7AT.

To supplement these 'official' reserves, we have in Britain a splendid tradition of voluntary organisations and the 41 County Trusts for Nature Conservation now between them own 1200 nature reserves throughout Britain, most of these purchased through the fund-raising efforts of the local Trust members. These reserves provide considerable protection for very many endangered species and threatened habitats, and more local reserves are acquired every week. For information on these reserves, and to help with this conservation effort in your area (all who care for the countryside should join their local County Trust), write to the Society for the Promotion of Nature Conservation (see above), the coordinating body for all the County Trusts.

The Royal Society for the Protection of Birds is another voluntary organisation with reserves. Naturally these are primarily for birds, but at many of them there are also interesting wild flowers to be seen. For information, contact the RSPB, The Lodge, Sandy, Bedfordshire SG19 2DL.

Of particular interest for wild flowers, many of the cornfield flowers which have now vanished from our farm fields are grown as part of the Iron Age farm reconstruction of the Butser Ancient Farm Project. Flowers such as corncockles and cornflowers can be seen here in the summer months growing in the fields with the ancient types of corn. For further information, write to the Butser Ancient Farm Demonstration Area, Queen Elizabeth County Park, Gravel Hill, Horndean, Portsmouth PO8 0QE.

A Selection of Species

The choice of the 50 species described and illustrated in the following pages was not an easy one. The most recently published standard list of British wild plants, J.E. Dandy's *List of British Vascular Plants* (1958), contains 2895 species and sub-species.

It was therefore decided to choose for this selection some of our most threatened wild flowers—spring gentian, fritillary, Snowdon lily and lady's-slipper—and some favourites which can still be easily found in Britain—heather, meadow buttercup, thrift and yellow iris— all of which can be seen in many country areas, although they are less common now than 100 years ago. A few from each of seven habitats have been chosen and the most distinctive characteristics of each plant are given as an aid to recognition; less obvious features have not been described for every plant. For those who wish to extend their knowledge of this subject, we include a list of the more comprehensive works available, in the chapter on identification.

The distribution maps on the following pages give a general summary of the approximate range of each species—in 1900 and at the present time. In many cases there has been a noticeable decrease in the areas in which the plants grow now as compared to the spread of those plants at the beginning of the century. In some species however, the decrease has been largely in *numbers* of plants—often a spectacular reduction—but at the same time a few plants still survive in many of the places where the species was formerly abundant. Therefore some of the areas marked on recent maps show plants which may still be seen occasionally—but in small numbers compared with past years.

These maps give an indication of the comparative distributions but are not intended to show precise presence or absence of individual plants. Some flowers may be found in areaswhich are left blank on the present distribution map of the species—and it is always exciting to find a plant uncommon to an area; these blank areas, therefore, can indicate populations known to be decreasing.

Remember: if you do find an unusual flower, leave it to grow in the wild to survive for all to enjoy.

To use the maps: diagonal lines indicate those areas of distribution in1900; solid areas indicate those areas of distribution of the present day.

Germander Speedwell

Veronica chamaedrys

Size: 6 – 15 in (20 – 40 cm).

Flowers: about 3/8 in (1 cm)
across; a bright deep blue with
a white eye; the stamens
projecting forwards and
conspicuous.

Leaves: about 3/8 in (1 cm)
long; triangular-oval and
without stalks; leaf margins
with rounded indentations.

Fruit: heart-shaped capsule.

Growth: stems with long
white hairs in two lines on
opposite sides of stem; lower
stems prostrate and often
rooting at the 'nodes' — where
the leaves join the stem.

Flowering time: March – July.

In hedgerows, woods and in grassland the
germander speedwell is widely distributed
throughout Britain, one of our favourite and
most familiar wild flowers. As a wayside
flower it was called 'speedwell' to 'speed you
well' on your journey; it is also known as
bird's-eye speedwell from the vivid blue of its
open flowers. Whereas this speedwell is
widespread in the countryside, some
mountain species of speedwell grow only
on high mountains in Scotland, and
others are restricted to some
sandy areas of East Anglia where
they are rare and in danger of
extinction but for conservation
measures to ensure their survival.
Other speedwells have been
introduced to Britain through
agriculture and horticulture, and
have spread widely to become
well established in our countryside; an example
of this is the common field speedwell, *Veronica
persica*.

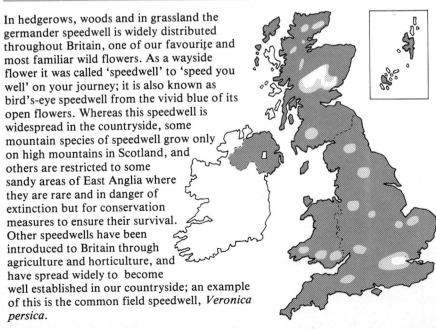

Silverweed

Potentilla anserina

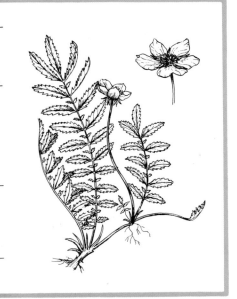

Size: to 30 in (80 cm).

Flowers: single flowers borne on long stalks; the flowers are open, 1 in (2.5 cm) across, with five bright yellow petals.

Leaves: pinnate with 7 – 12 pairs of leaflets arranged in two rows along the stalk. Each leaflet up to 2 1/2 in (6 cm), oval, with margins deeply toothed with narrow teeth, and covered with silky hairs.

Growth: a prostrate plant; the thick rootstock has a rosette of leaves and long creeping stolons which root again at intervals and bear the flowers.

Flowering time: June – August.

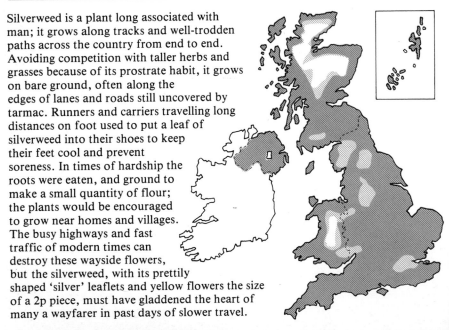

Silverweed is a plant long associated with man; it grows along tracks and well-trodden paths across the country from end to end. Avoiding competition with taller herbs and grasses because of its prostrate habit, it grows on bare ground, often along the edges of lanes and roads still uncovered by tarmac. Runners and carriers travelling long distances on foot used to put a leaf of silverweed into their shoes to keep their feet cool and prevent soreness. In times of hardship the roots were eaten, and ground to make a small quantity of flour; the plants would be encouraged to grow near homes and villages. The busy highways and fast traffic of modern times can destroy these wayside flowers, but the silverweed, with its prettily shaped 'silver' leaflets and yellow flowers the size of a 2p piece, must have gladdened the heart of many a wayfarer in past days of slower travel.

Greater Stitchwort

Stellaria holostea

Size: 6 – 15 in (15 – 60 cm).

Flowers: 3/8 in (1.5 cm) across; a few flowers in a loose head on stalks up to 4 in (10 cm). Petals white, divided to halfway down centre lengthwise. Sepals green with narrow white papery margins.

Fruit: capsule about 1/4 in (7 mm); almost globular.

Leaves: 1/4 – 3/8 in (0.5 – 1 cm); narrow, lance shaped with a fine tapering point and with rough margins; leaf surfaces smooth and slightly blue-green.

Growth: slender stems; weak, brittle and with four angles.

Flowering time: April – June.

The greater stitchwort is typically a plant of woodlands where it can be found growing throughout Britain. It is also a plant of hedgerows as the shade and shelter provided by a well-maintained hedge give very similar conditions for the growth of small plants as in a mixed wood or along woodland rides. Many miles of hedgerow have been uprooted and destroyed in recent years – this has resulted in a considerable loss of suitable habitat for greater stitchwort and others. Whiter than almost any other British wild flower, the petals shine from spring-green grass – at dusk too they can especially catch the eye. The divided petals resemble embroidery, suitable to its name, although this more likely refers to the plant being used to cure a stitch or sharp pricking pain.

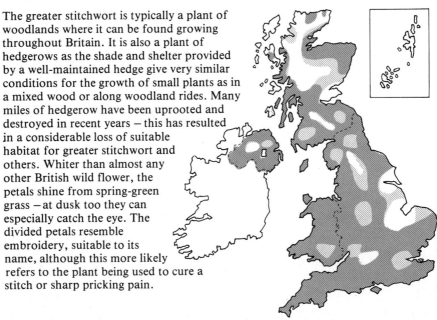

Scarlet Pimpernel

Anagallis arvensis

Size: to 12 in (30 cm)

Flowers: flat, open, 1/2 in (14 cm); on slender stems with 5 overlapping broad oval petals. Petals usually scarlet red, but blue, pink or yellow occur.

Fruit: globular capsule, 1/4 in (5 mm) diameter

Leaves: 3/4 – 1 1/4 in (2 – 3 cm) oval, without stalks.

Growth: plants usually prostrate; stems square.

Flowering time: June – September.

Other details: stems and leaves are dotted with tiny black glands, and each petal is fringed with glandular hairs.

Mainly a weed of cultivation, the scarlet pimpernel is one of those wild flowers no longer found in arable fields: the screening of the farmer's seeds and the use of sprays has largely removed the weeds from fields growing crops. It does however grow frequently on coastal sand dunes, on waste ground and sometimes as a garden weed. It is rare in the far north of Britain. The petals are very sensitive to changes of humidity in the atmosphere; the flowers close in damp weather to reopen in sunshine, giving the plant its country name of 'poor man's weatherglass'. The closing of the flowers is an adaptation by which the pollen grains are exposed only when the air is dry, being protected from the damp by the closing petals.

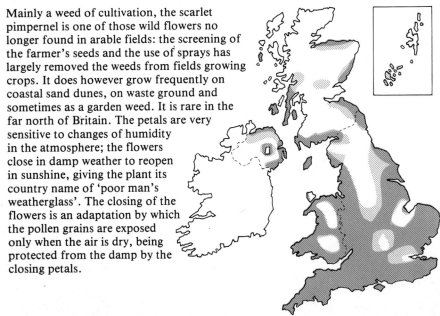

Cow Parsley

Anthriscus sylvestris

Size: to 3 feet (1 m).

Flowers: minute 1/8 – 3/16 in (3 – 4 mm), white; in flat heads made up of groups of flowers on a number of branching, rayed stalks.

Leaves: 12 in (30 cm); finely cut with rounded segments.

Fruit: see drawing. Each species in this family has a characteristic fruit of great diagnostic importance.

Distribution: in hedgerows, along roadside verges — where not too frequently mown — and wood edges. This is the most widespread of the spring- flowering umbellifers in southern England.

Flowering time: April – June.

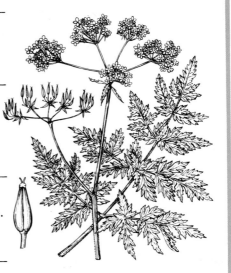

Cow parsley is seen along our roadsides in spring and summer, sometimes as an edging of billowing white flowerheads. Other plants of this family, looking similar, flower at other seasons, in different parts of Britain or in other types of habitat. Cow parsley was formerly a common plant of meadows — its name associates it with cows — but with changes in farming practice few meadows now have a natural selection of wild flowers through the summer. Other country names, 'Queen Anne's lace' and 'lady's lace', describe the dainty outline of these plants with their tiny flower and filigree leaves. This family includes many plants useful to man, especially aromatic herbs, e.g. caraway, fennel and dill; but it also includes some very poisonous plants such as hemlock and hemlock water-dropwort.

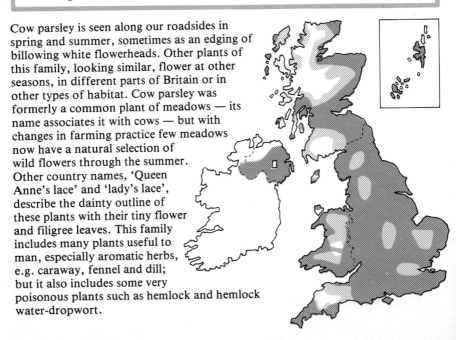

Red Campion

Silene dioica

Size: 12 – 36 in (30 – 90 cm).

Flowers: 3/4 – 1 in (2 – 2.5 cm) across, with short stalks in many-flowered heads. Petals bright rose-pink, divided deeply into two narrow segments.

Fruit: capsule opening when ripe by 10 revolute teeth, to release the black seeds.

Leaves: basal leaves oval and narrowed into a long winged stalk; upper leaves oval oblong without, or only very short, stalk.

Growth: whole plant covered with soft hairs, and may be slightly sticky.

Flowering time: May – June.

As with the greater stitchwort, this is a woodland plant which can be found frequently in hedgerows where these are still in existence. When growing in woods the red campion is particularly found in clearings, at wood edges, and in well-drained woods on limestone. The distribution throughout Britain is patchy — in some areas it is locally abundant, but is very rare in others. It requires base-rich soils with good drainage, and colonises specialised habitats such as mountain scree slopes where these are sufficiently stabilised, and on ledges on bird cliffs by the sea where the red campion is often to be seen growing on the nitrate-rich soil amongst the sea-birds' nests. In the West Country it is common on road verges — particularly where roads are edged by earthed walls or sloping banks; here red campion flowers can colour the roadsides.

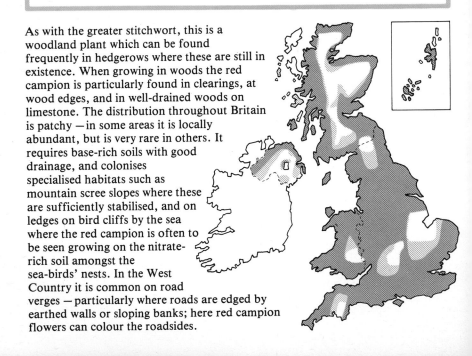

Traveller's-joy

Clematis vitalba

Size: to 100 ft (30 m).

Flowers: 3/4 in (2 cm) across in clustered heads. False petals greenish white and very hairy on the backs. No true petals. Many stamens.

Fruit: very conspicuous. Clusters of achenes with long 2 1/2 in (6 cm) feathery styles.

Leaves: pinnate with usually 4 rather distant leaflets; leaflets 2 – 4 in (5 – 10 cm) narrowly oval, pointed at the tip and rounded at the base.

Growth: perennial climbing shrub with tough woody stems.

Flowering time: July – September; fruits persisting into winter months.

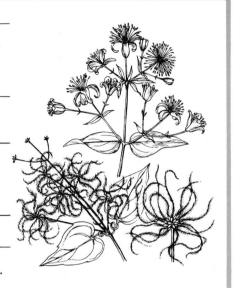

A fragrant plant of central and southern England and Wales only, it is restricted to calcareous soils or rocks and is very commonly found on downland in thickets and scrambling over other shrubs and small trees on chalk soils. Traveller's-joy also frequently occurs in roadside hedgerows, even along roads crossing areas of weald and clay, because chalk was frequently used to stabilise the surface and side banks of roads when highways were constructed over clay soils. The name 'traveller's-joy' is attributed to Gerard in his famous *Herbal* of 1597; he described the plant as 'decking and adorning waies and hedges', and still today travellers in autumn along the roads of southern Britain can delight in the feathery fruits garlanding roadside shrubs and hedgerows.

Common Poppy

Papaver rhoeas

Size: 8 – 25 in (20 – 60 cm).

Flowers: 2 3/4 – 4 in (7 – 10 cm) across; petals roundish, soft in texture and often somewhat wrinkled. Flowers scarlet, sometimes with black blotch at base of each petal giving a black centre to the flower; flower stalks hairy; sepals bristly.

Fruit: capsule to 5/8 in (1.5 cm); without hairs; oval or rounded.

Leaves: basal leaves stalked and divided; upper leaves without stalks.

Growth: usually branched.

Flowering time: June – August.

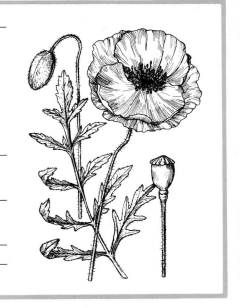

One of the traditional cornfield weeds, the common poppy was largely eliminated from arable fields by the use of herbicides. As these increase in cost however, their use is sometimes more restricted, and scarlet poppies can be seen in the fields in some areas. The seed of the common poppy is particularly adapted to survival for many years — the seeds remain viable through a long dormancy period below the soil of undisturbed ground and very large numbers of seeds are produced by each poppy plant. The four species of poppy native to our countryside may all be distinguished by the shape and hairiness of their capsules. Each capsule may hold 1300 seeds and an average plant will produce 17000 seeds in one growing season.

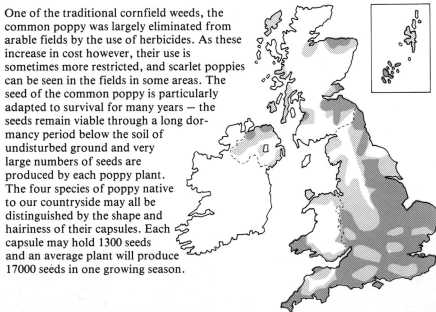

Lords-and-Ladies

Arum maculatum

Size: 12 – 20 in (30 – 50 cm).

Flowers: first shows as a green pointed spike up to 1 ft (30 cm) high; this unfurls into a green or purple-spotted spathe ensheathing a dull-purple, or sometimes yellow, spadix.

Fruit: stout spike of bright orange-scarlet berries, in September – October.

Leaves: to 8 in (20 cm) with long stalk; smooth, long triangular, dark green, often with blackish spots.

Growth: from an underground tuber, from which a fresh plant grows each year.

Flowering time: April – May.

Lords-and-ladies has been common as a plant of our decreasing hedgerows. It is also a plant of woodlands on base-rich soils, and is very tolerant of shade. It is generally distributed through England, Wales and Ireland, but uncommon in Scotland. These have a unique and very specialised pollination mechanism. The ripening spadix releases a scent, not obvious to humans but readily detected by, and very compelling to, some small insects, especially moth-flies. These 'home-in' on the scent and crawl down the spadix through a ring of long downward-pointing hairs into the enclosure at the base. The hairs prevent immediate escape, but, after the plant has been pollinated by the crawling insects, the hairs shrivel, releasing the creatures unharmed.
As the berries ripen the spathe and spadix above wither and drop, leaving the poisonous orange-scarlet berries at the top of the stem.

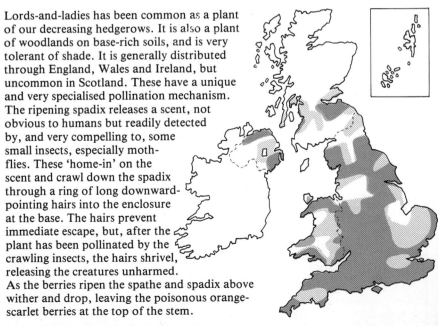

Herb Robert

Geranium robertianum

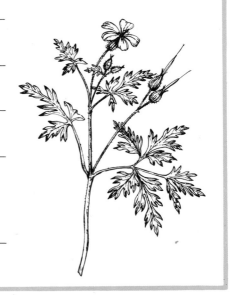

Size: 4 – 20 in (10 – 50 cm).

Flowers: 3/4 in (2 cm) across, bright pink; petals rounded at tip and rather separated.

Leaves: shaped as polygons, with five deeply cut leaflets; slightly hairy.

Fruit: to 3/4 in (2 cm), with beaks; sometimes stiffly hairy, and usually held erect when ripe.

Growth: branched from the base; stems fragile; stems and leaves usually reddish. The plant has a strongly disagreeable smell when crushed.

Flowering time: May – September.

Herb robert is tolerant of several different kinds of habitat. It is a plant of woods, hedgebanks and waysides; it also grows on mountain rocks and on coastal shingle beaches. Two sub-species have been differentiated from the common type by their different growth forms — a rather rare small seaside form and a Celtic plant which grows on sunny limestone rocks in Wales. Herb robert has long been a familiar plant of the odd corners of garden and village and was well known to our ancestors. This can be seen by the very long list of over 100 country names which were used for herb robert in different parts of Britain. The name, herb robert, is most likely associated with Robin Goodfellow — the house goblin linked with mischief and sly pranks.

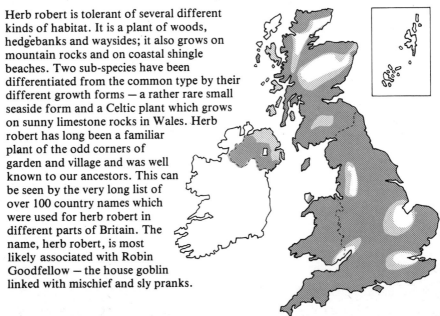

Cowslip

Primula veris

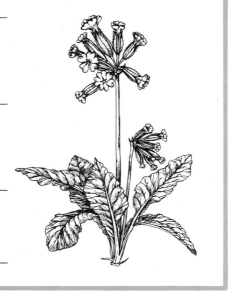

Size: 4 – 12 in (10 – 30 cm).

Flowers: 3/8 – 5/8 in (1.0 – 1.5 cm) across; golden-yellow with orange spot at base of petal lobes; the flowers funnel-shaped, lower part enclosed by pale green calyx tube.

Leaves: 6 in (15 cm); oblong to oval, blunt at tip; leaf blades abruptly contracted into leaf stalk; both surfaces of leaf wrinkled, and with downy hairs.

Growth: leaves at ground level growing from top of rootstock; flower stems erect, with flowers stalked and nodding.

Flowering time: April – May.

A plant of calcareous or basic soils, the cowslip grows especially in old pastures, on downland and on sand dunes. Except in a few Scottish counties, cowslips were formerly found throughout Britain, and often they were locally abundant. In recent years most pasture land in this country has been ploughed and re-seeded to improve the grassland for grazing; many acres of downland too have come under the plough — once the turf has been ploughed the cowslips cannot survive. Railway embankments when scythed were often noted for displays of cowslip flowers in spring; but modern labour-saving management with herbicides has destroyed many miles of cowslips on railway banks.

In 1975 a campaign was launched to save some old pasture in each county before it is too late.

Green-winged Orchid

Orchis morio

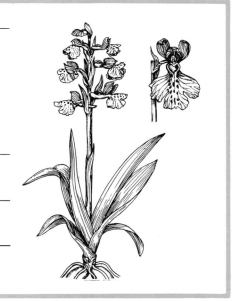

Size: 4 – 16 in (10 – 40 cm).

Flowers: the 3 upper segments are joined to form a helmet-shaped hood which has conspicuous green veins (from which it gets its name); the lip 3-lobed, broader than long, about equalling the hood in length. Purple, but may be pale pink or white.

Leaves: 1 – 4 in (3 – 9 cm) long, 1/8 – 5/8 in (0.5 – 1.5 cm) wide; oblong to lanceolate.

Growth: lower leaves spreading or recurved, upper leaves appressed to flower stem.

Flowering time: May – June.

This orchid grows in meadows and pastures, especially on calcareous soils. Like the cowslip, it is a plant which cannot survive ploughing; where it was formerly abundant, it has become increasingly scarce through modern changes in farm practice. The green-winged orchid has been recorded in churchyards where it can survive with suitable maintenance regimes — highlighting the value of churchyards as oases for wildlife conservation. The colour variation in the flowers can range from dark purple (almost black) through deep and pale pinks to the occasional white spike — flowering in mass this orchid can be a breath-taking sight. The unspotted leaves and green veins on the hood distinguish it from the early-purple orchid which has black spotted leaves. Please remember that wild orchids should *never* be picked.

Meadow Buttercup

Ranunculus acris

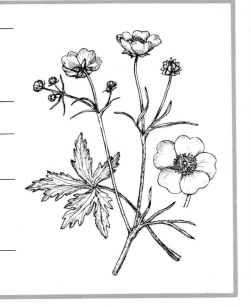

Size: 6 – 40 in (15 – 100 cm).

Flowers: 3/4 – 1 in (2.0 – 2.5 cm) across; bright glossy golden yellow; open flowers with a mass of yellowish stamens.

Fruit: a cluster of small green shiny nut-like achenes.

Leaves: basal and lower stem leaves, long stalked and pentagonal in outline.

Growth: the wiry flower stems are loosely branched, each terminating in a small cluster of buds, of which a single one flowers at one time.

Flowering time: May – August.

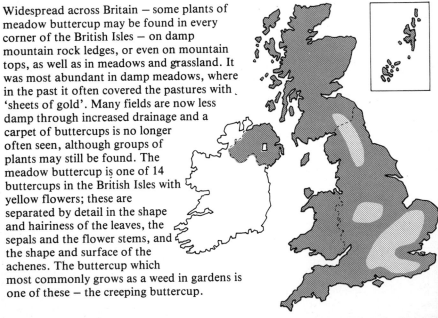

Widespread across Britain — some plants of meadow buttercup may be found in every corner of the British Isles — on damp mountain rock ledges, or even on mountain tops, as well as in meadows and grassland. It was most abundant in damp meadows, where in the past it often covered the pastures with 'sheets of gold'. Many fields are now less damp through increased drainage and a carpet of buttercups is no longer often seen, although groups of plants may still be found. The meadow buttercup is one of 14 buttercups in the British Isles with yellow flowers; these are separated by detail in the shape and hairiness of the leaves, the sepals and the flower stems, and the shape and surface of the achenes. The buttercup which most commonly grows as a weed in gardens is one of these — the creeping buttercup.

Fritillary

Fritillaria meleagris

Size: 8 – 20 in (20 – 50 cm).

Flowers: about 2 in (5 cm); no true petals, but oblong perianth segments forming a nodding bell-shaped flower; perianth chequered, dark and pale dull purple; glistening nectaries at the base of the inner surfaces.

Fruit: a rounded capsule.

Leaves: shiny, blue-green, narrow and grass-like.

Growth: from a bulb; flowers single, or sometimes paired.

Flowering time: April – May.

This plant of damp meadows in southern Britain has dramatically decreased in the last 30 years. Always a local plant, with specialised habitat requirements, it did, however, grow in abundance in some fields; for example, a few places in Wiltshire, Suffolk and the riverside meadows in Oxford were famed for their fritillaries. It is also grown in gardens — a few plants that escape from gardens become naturalised and are reported from time to time. But of the 93 truly native sites known in 1950, less than ten remained in 1979. Swift action was necessary to avert possible complete extinction of these native plants; several sites are now Nature Reserves. The Fox Fritillary Meadow Reserve in Framsden, Suffolk has an open day in April each year to give an opportunity to see the wonderful sight of a field of flowering fritillaries, or 'snake's heads' as they are sometimes called.

Wood-sorrel

Oxalis acetosella

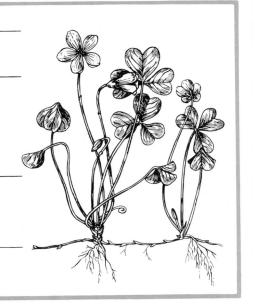

Size: 2 – 6 in (5 – 15 cm).

Flowers: 3/5 – 5/8 in
(1.0 – 1.5 cm), nodding; petals
white, veined with lilac.

Leaves: trifoliate, the three
leaflets on stalks up to 6 in (15
cm) long; each leaflet
3/8 – 3/4 in (1 – 2 cm),
broader than long, with
smooth margin; the leaflets a
clear yellow-green.

Growth: clusters of leaf stalks
grow from a creeping rhizome;
only one flower on each flower
stalk at about the same height
as leaflets.

Flowering time: April – May.

This delicate little plant grows mainly in
woodlands. It is very tolerant of shade, and
may carpet the ground in beech woods, some
oak woods or mixed woodland. It grows on
lighter soils, often in the leaf humus under the
trees; it may also be found growing in the
moss covering the trunks of older and
branched trees. Wood-sorrel may also grow in
hedgerows and on shady rocks on mountains. It is sometimes a shy
flowerer, but the fresh green trefoil
leaves can be conspicuous in the
ground-cover vegetation
throughout the summer. When it
is in flower, the tracery of the
lilac veins inside the petals may be
seen by gently tilting a single
flower upwards. The wood-
sorrel is the only native *Oxalis* in
Britain, but many introduced
species of this family, with yellow or pink
flowers, grow as weeds in our gardens.

Herb-Paris

Paris quadrifolia

Size: 8 – 16 in (20 – 40 cm).

Flowers: 2 – 3 in (5 – 7 cm) across; green star-like, usually with four narrow awl-shaped petals about 1 in (2.5 cm) and slightly longer sepals.

Fruit: a single fleshy capsule, round and berry-like, black when ripe.

Leaves: typically 4, but occasionally from 3 – 8; 2 1/2 – 5 in (6 – 12 cm).

Growth: the leaf arrangement is very striking, being in a single whorl near the top of the stem, and topped by the single flower.

Flowering time: May – August.

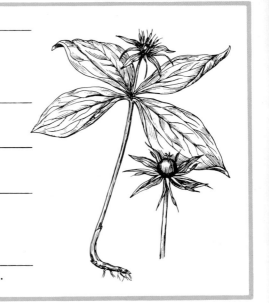

This curious flower is not common in Britain, but is found occasionally in damp woods on calcareous soils. In the south it may be under beech trees on chalk; in the north in woodlands on limestone rocks where it grows under ash and wych elm trees. Where the limestone is fissured to form 'limestone pavement', the crevices, or 'grykes', offer damp and shade similar to a woodland habitat and herb-paris is one of the plants typically growing in these grykes. In Wales there are some woods where herb-paris grows under small-leaved lime trees, but this flower is less common in the west of Britain and entirely absent from Ireland and the Scottish islands. The flower parts are usually regularly in fours, and from this gets its name, 'herba paris', as the herb of equality (from the Latin meaning 'equal' or 'pair'). The berry is poisonous.

Primrose

Primula vulgaris

Size: to 4 in (10 cm).

Flowers: about 1 in (3 cm) across; pale yellow, with deeper yellow centre. Petals ¾ in (1.5 cm), with shallow notch; calyx pale green, pleated, nearly tubular and with long shaggy hairs. Scented.

Leaves: 4 – 8 in (10 – 20 cm); stalkless; oval, blunt at tip and gradually narrowing to base; the margin irregularly toothed; upper surface almost hairless and somewhat wrinkled, softly hairy beneath.

Growth: loosely tufted plants; the flowers just overtopping the clumps of leaves.

Flowering time: March – May. They may flower earlier, especially in the south-west.

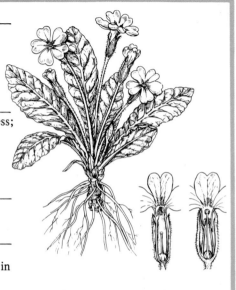

A welcome symbol of springtime, the primrose holds a special place in the affections of all those with an eye for the countryside. The temptation to take wild plants to grow in the garden has been strong, and recent surveys show that the primrose is disappearing rapidly from the vicinity of all our major towns and cities. We must all leave primroses in the wild for everyone, and for future generations, to enjoy. The primrose grows generally throughout Britain, but less commonly in the north. It is a flower of woodlands, of hedgebanks and railway banks; in the west it also grows in open grassy places, on sheltered cliffs and sometimes down to the edge of the sea. Occasional pink- flowered plants are garden forms which have escaped from cultivation, but in a few woodlands in Wales pink primroses are thought to be native.

Bluebell

Endymion non-scriptus

Size: 8 – 20 in (20 – 50 cm).

Flowers: blue; ⅝ – ¾ in (1.5 – 2.0 cm); bell-shaped, with perianth segments joined at the base and recurved at the tips. Usually 5 – 20 in a one-sided inflorescence at top of stem, which droops at the tip.

Leaves: narrow, linear, 8 – 18 in (20 – 45 cm) long, 3/8 – 5/8 in (1.0 – 1.5 cm) wide.

Growth: from bulb. Each flower on a short stalk, about 3/16 in (0.5 cm), and with a pair of short leaf-like bracts opposite.

Flowering time: April – June.

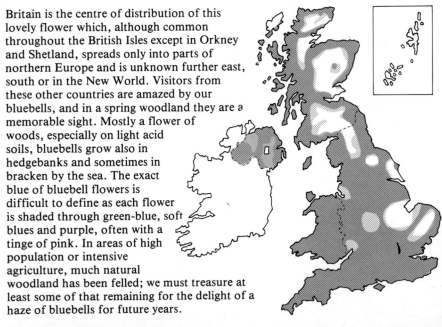

Britain is the centre of distribution of this lovely flower which, although common throughout the British Isles except in Orkney and Shetland, spreads only into parts of northern Europe and is unknown further east, south or in the New World. Visitors from these other countries are amazed by our bluebells, and in a spring woodland they are a memorable sight. Mostly a flower of woods, especially on light acid soils, bluebells grow also in hedgebanks and sometimes in bracken by the sea. The exact blue of bluebell flowers is difficult to define as each flower is shaded through green-blue, soft blues and purple, often with a tinge of pink. In areas of high population or intensive agriculture, much natural woodland has been felled; we must treasure at least some of that remaining for the delight of a haze of bluebells for future years.

Wood Anemone

Anemone nemorosa

Size: 4 – 20 in (10 – 25 cm).

Flowers: 3/4 – 1 1/2 in (2 – 4 cm) across; no petals; sepals white, hairless and often tinged on the back with pink; a mass of many (50 – 70) golden stamens in the centre of flower.

Fruit: 10 – 30 downy achenes in a rounded cluster.

Leaves: from the rhizome, one or two leaves appear after flowering; long, stalked, three-lobed and again divided.

Growth: the unbranched stem bears stem leaves two-thirds of the way up, and a single terminal flower.

Flowering time: March – May.

A woodland plant which is tolerant of most soils, the wood anemone grows in all but very acid or water-logged sites, and in deciduous woods. It can be found throughout Britain except for the Outer Hebrides, Orkney and Shetland and some of the smaller islands without trees. It is also not found in Ireland or the Channel Islands. Some shelter is necessary for this slender plant, for which another name is the 'windflower', describing its nodding movement in the slightest breeze. When trees in a woodland are thinned, in the first subsequent years the extra light encourages increased flowering of the wood anemones, but the upturned white-gold or drooping pink flowers do not survive for many years in open ground without shade and shelter.

The wood anemone is the only true anemone growing wild in Britain of the several anemone species in continental Europe.

Purple-loosestrife

Lythrum salicaria

Size: 24 – 48 in (60 – 120 cm).

Flowers: in dense spikes of many flowers up to 12 in (30 cm) in length; each flower about 1/2 in (1.5 cm) across, arranged in whorls in the axils of leaf-like bracts.

Leaves: 2 – 3 in (5 – 7 cm); stalkless spear-shaped with pointed tip and heart-shaped base. Lower leaves sometimes opposite in pairs, or in whorls of three; upper leaves usually alternate.

Growth: a perennial plant with many erect, slender stems.

Flowering time: June – September.

A plant of wet places, purple-loosestrife can be seen among reeds and rushes around lake margins (a habitat known as a 'reed-swamp'), and along the banks of slow-moving rivers. Also in marshes and fens, it often forms large stands, especially colourful if the purple spikes are seen against a background of blue water. This is a plant of the south and west in Britain, becoming less frequent in Scotland and it is entirely absent from the far north. It can be locally abundant, forming large stands of purple, impressive when in full flower. With each year, as more of our land is drained, there are fewer marshes and damp fields, and the water table in general is lower, so that, as a consequence, the areas of colourful displays of marsh plants become fewer and less often seen.

Arrowhead

Sagittaria sagittifolia

Size: 12 – 36 in (30 – 90 cm).

Flowers: in whorls of 3 to 5, each flower about 1 in (2 cm) across; the pure white sepals have a conspicuous dark violet patch at the base.

Fruit: nearly spherical heads of nutlets, 1/2 in (1.5 cm) across.

Leaves: three forms: submerged leaves narrow and linear; floating leaves spear-shaped to oval; above the water, long stalked with characteristic arrow-shaped blade.

Growth: in water, with flower stem and aerial leaves held above water surface.

Flowering time: July – September.

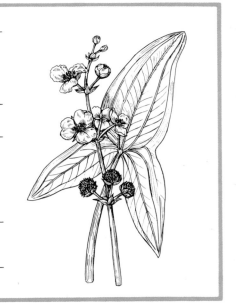

Arrowhead grows in shallow water, in ponds, canals and slow-flowing rivers with a muddy bed in which the plants root. Records for this plant are scattered through England, Wales and the north of Ireland, but it is not generally common. This interesting plant is attractive at all stages – before the flowers open the buds are spherical and shiny green; the wide open, comparatively large but short-lived white flowers with violet centres are lovely above clear water; the anthers of the stamens in the violet centres are also arrow-shaped. The almost-rounded heads of fruits are distinctive, too, spiked and knobby, and sometimes buds and flowers and fruit can be seen together on one stem. The leaves are also of special interest with three distinct forms on the same plant.

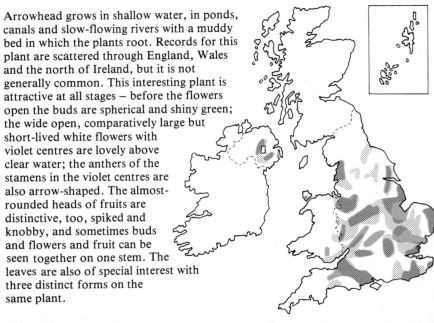

Marsh-marigold

Caltha palustris

Size: 4 – 8 in (10 – 20 cm).

Flowers: 1 – 2 in (2 – 5 cm) across; 5 sepals, bright golden yellow above, greenish-yellow below; no petals; many (up to 100) golden stamens.

Fruit: up to 10 clustered pod-like carpels, 1/2 – 1 in (1 – 2.5 cm), splitting along one side to release seeds.

Leaves: rounded or kidney-shaped with heart-shaped base; lower leaves long stalked, upper smaller and stalkless under flowers.

Growth: a stout perennial, hairless and shiny.

Flowering time: March – July.

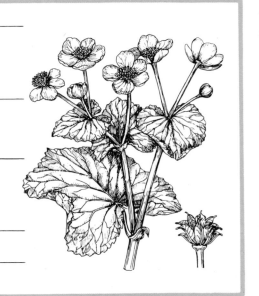

Marsh-marigolds grow in wet and water-logged places, especially where there is some shade. It may be found in marshes, wet woods, ditches and in fens — but not on very acid peat. It grows also on damp mountain meadows and along the becks and burns of uplands and mountains in northern England and Scotland; here it may be one of the first plants to grow through melting snow. Spring-flowering in the lowlands and the south, plants growing high on mountains may only just be in flower in late summer. The marsh-marigold is a plant which has markedly suffered through land drainage, especially in lowland Britain. Comparatively recently, wide splashes of the golden flowers were a familar sight to travellers through the countryside in spring, but there are now many areas in the Home Counties where only an occasional marsh-marigold can be seen today.

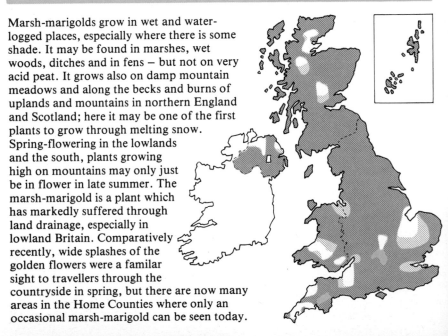

Marsh Helleborine

Epipactis palustris

Size: 8 – 18 in (20 – 45 cm).

Flowers: 7 – 15 flowers in a stalked spike with the flowers more or less turned to one side and drooping in bud. Each flower about 1/2 in (1.5 cm); sepals purplish-brown; two narrow petals, white flushed or veined with crimson; lip white usually with some crimson and a yellow patch.

Fruit: a drooping capsule with downy hairs.

Leaves: narrow with acute tip, keeled and folded; lower leaves 2 – 6 in (5 – 15 cm).

Growth: stems erect and wiry.

Flowering time: June – August.

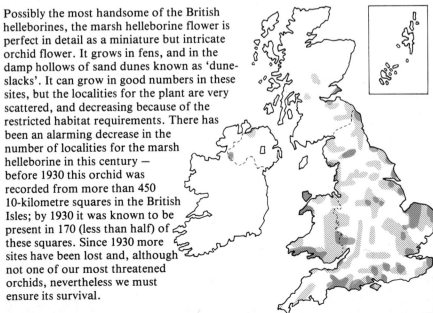

Possibly the most handsome of the British helleborines, the marsh helleborine flower is perfect in detail as a miniature but intricate orchid flower. It grows in fens, and in the damp hollows of sand dunes known as 'dune-slacks'. It can grow in good numbers in these sites, but the localities for the plant are very scattered, and decreasing because of the restricted habitat requirements. There has been an alarming decrease in the number of localities for the marsh helleborine in this century — before 1930 this orchid was recorded from more than 450 10-kilometre squares in the British Isles; by 1930 it was known to be present in 170 (less than half) of these squares. Since 1930 more sites have been lost and, although not one of our most threatened orchids, nevertheless we must ensure its survival.

Hemlock Water-dropwort

Oenanthe crocata

Size: 20 – 60 in (50 – 150 cm).

Flowers: a rounded many-rayed umbel of very tiny white flowers, 1/16 in (2 mm) across. Outer petals longer than inner.

Fruit: 1/8 – 1/4 in (4 – 6 mm), cylindrical, with styles remaining erect at top (see drawing).

Leaves: to 16 in (40 cm), stalked, with base of stalk sheathing stem; blade large and deltoid and dissected 3 or 4 times into rounded segments.

Growth: stems hollow, grooved and branched.

Flowering time: June – July.

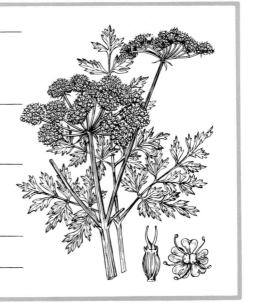

This plant of wet places is restricted to the south, south-west and western edges of Britain. Here it grows fairly commonly along rivers, streams and in roadside ditches. It can be a spectacular roadside plant where there is a damp ditch following the line of the highway, until, as is so often the practice today, the water is piped and the ditches levelled. It is a plant which grows mainly on neutral or acid soils, and is only infrequently found by chalk streams. The white-flowered plants of the umbellifer family are very difficult to distinguish one from another. The hemlock water-dropwort is virulently poisonous, and the greatest care should be taken in handling the plants, no part of which should ever be eaten.

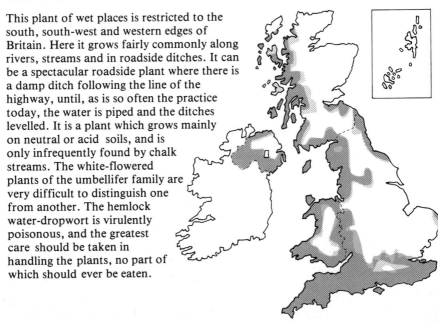

Bog Asphodel

Narthecium ossifragum

Size: 3 – 16 in (7 – 40 cm).

Flowers: yellow, star-shaped, in a spike of up to 4 in (10 cm) at top of stem. Each flower 3/5 – 4/5 in (1.5 – 2.0 cm) across, with 6 narrow petals, centred by a tuft of stamens with orange anthers and stalks with long woolly hairs.

Fruit: deep reddish-orange capsules 1/2 in (12 mm).

Leaves: flattened basal tuft of curved, rigid narrow leaves 2 – 12 in (5 – 30 cm) long.

Growth: hairless; flower spike higher than leaves.

Flowering time: June – September.

This plant of bogs and wet, acid places grows on mountains and heaths. It can be found across most of Scotland, Northern Ireland and the Welsh mountains, but it is largely absent from a large part of central, eastern and south-eastern England. In some areas it grows in quantity, sometimes flowering and fruiting together to give a spectacular display of yellow, orange and bright green leaves — often against black peat. It is decreasing and disappearing fast from many of its remaining sites — by 1930 it had become extinct in East Anglia in all but three of its recorded localities as damp heathland was drained, primarily for afforestation. The bog asphodel is a typical plant of wild landscapes which were at one time impractical for cultivation but, with modern machinery, are now used for forestry and agriculture.

Bog Pimpernel

Anagallis tenella

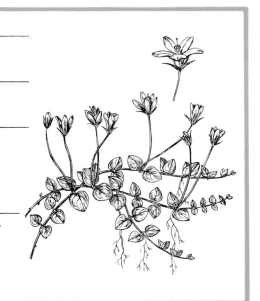

Size: 2 – 6 in (5 – 15 cm).

Flowers: funnel-shaped,
1/5 – 2/5 in (0.5 – 1.0 cm);
delicate shell-pink.

Leaves: tiny, paired, rounded
oval leaves, 1/4 in (5 mm)
long, with very short stalks.

Growth: slender, hairless,
with prostrate creeping stems
rooting freely at the nodes.
Flowers held above the leaves
on very slender thread-like
stalks.

Flowering time: June – August.

This pretty plant grows in damp and grassy
places and in peat bogs. It is frequent only in
the south-west, along our western coasts and
offshore islands. Again, this is a plant which is
decreasing as marsh and bog areas are
drained; by 1930, it was extinct in many
former localities in the south-east. In
Middlesex, for example, the bog pimpernel
was known in four places (abundantly so in one of these) just over
100 years ago, but its last sighting
in that county was in 1873 — it
must now be presumed to have
gone from Middlesex forever.
This small creeping plant is
seldom one that can be seen from
a distance as a feature of the
landscape, but it would be a sad
loss were it no longer a
British plant.

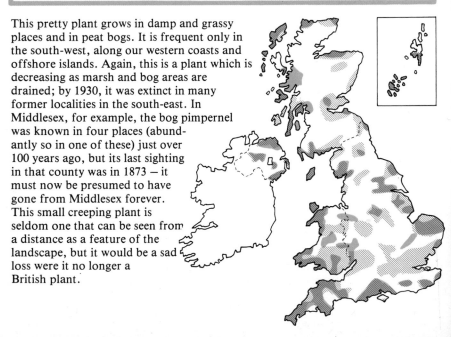

Yellow Iris

Iris pseudacorus

Size: 15 – 60 in (40 – 150 cm).

Flowers: 1 – 3 large, showy, yellow, 4 in (10 cm) across; 3 broad petals, spreading downwards (the 'falls'), veined and often with orange spot near base; 3 narrow erect, sometimes twisted, petals and 3 branched stigmas — all yellow.

Fruit: large elliptic capsule; brown seeds.

Leaves: 3/5 – 1 in (1.5 – 2.5 cm) wide, flat, sword-shaped with raised mid-rib.

Growth: from thickened rhizome; plant hairless.

Flowering time: May – July.

Yellow irises grow in marshes, in the shallow water at the edges of ponds and lakes, in wet woods and along the banks of rivers and ditches. Although it is still widely distributed in suitable habitats throughout most of Britain, except in the higher uplands, this again is a plant that has decreased in numbers with the draining of wetlands, especially in the south and west, where areas of damp meadows which intersect dikes, often known as 'levels' or 'wildbrooks', have been claimed for intensive agriculture. Known by its country name of 'yellow flag', it has been a familiar plant to generations of countrymen and poets. The bright flowers are a cheerful sight; the yellow, veined, pointed buds, too, are attractive, unfurling from the green sheathing spathe which splits as the flowers open.

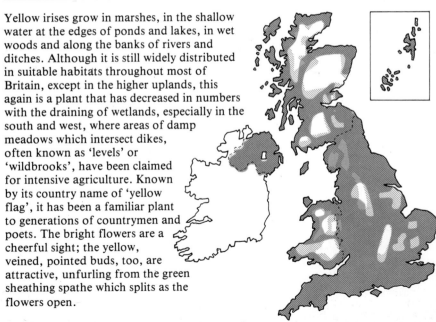

Mountain Pansy

Viola lutea

Size: 4 – 8 in (10 – 20 cm).

Flowers: flattened, with petals arranged in typical pansy 'face', 4/5 – 2/5 in (2.0 – 3.5 cm) in height with projecting spur at back of petals. Mostly yellow, with some brown 'honey-guide' veining on lower petals; some flowers purple or mixed.

Leaves: basal leaves broadly oval, upper leaves narrow and 2/5 – 4/5 in (1 – 2 cm) long; all stalked and with rounded toothed margins.

Growth: slender plants from a creeping rhizome; a succession of flowers on each plant.

Flowering: May – August.

This plant of mountain and hill grassland can be found growing at heights up to 3500 ft (1090 m). It is restricted to the mountain areas of Scotland, Wales, Cumbria and the Pennines, where it grows on base-rich soils, but is absent from the Lowlands, Northern Ireland, Orkney, Shetland and other islands. Garden pansies are familiar favourites, and the miniature wild pansies always attract attention and give pleasure. It is thought that our large-flowered garden varieties originated from a hybrid between the mountain pansy and the wild pansy of cultivated fields, *Viola tricolor* (or heart's-ease). This is an instance of the value of wild plants as stock from which new varieties may be selectively bred, or may arise spontaneously from time to time.

Wild Thyme

Thymus drucei

Size: a prostrate creeping plant up to 4 in (10 cm).

Flowers: in rounded heads of whorls of small flowers, at ends of branches. Flowers pink or rose-purple, bell-shaped, with petals divided into upper and lower lips; toothed calyx tube and 4 protruding stamens.

Leaves: very small, paired 1/6 – 1/3 in (4 – 8 mm) long, usually rounded to oval with short stalks, hairy.

Growth: mat-forming, usually with flower stems in rows on the branches. Plants aromatic.

Flowering time: May – August.

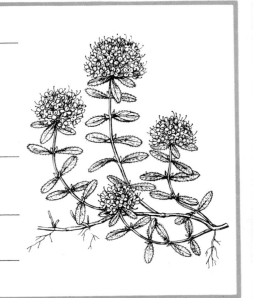

This plant of dry habitats grows in grassland, on heaths and dunes, and on rocks and screes. It is widespread throughout Britain, although less common in Ireland and in parts of East Anglia. It may grow with other closely-related species of thyme which vary in the hairiness of the leaves, arrangement of the hairs along the stems, or the shape of the flowerheads. These are difficult to distinguish, but it is said that grazing sheep can differentiate between them and will eat only selected plants of wild thyme. Some species are more aromatic than others — perhaps some of these are too spicy for the sheep. Wild thyme is very much associated with the Downs and with upland pastures where turf is short, and where the scent of thyme on the breeze on warm sunny days is evocative.

Common Rock-rose

Helianthemum chamaecistus

Size: 4 – 10 in (10 – 25 cm).

Flowers: about 1 in (2.5 cm) across when open; up to 12 in a loosely branched inflorescence. Petals pale golden or sulphur-yellow, sometimes with orange spot at the base. Inner sepals pale with very prominent green veins.

Leaves: oval or oblong, with only one vein; 1/5 – 4/5 in (0.5 – 2.0 cm) long. Rather dark green and shiny above, white with downy hairs below; paired, and with small stipules.

Growth: from a woody stock, stems branched and straggling.

Flowering time: June – September.

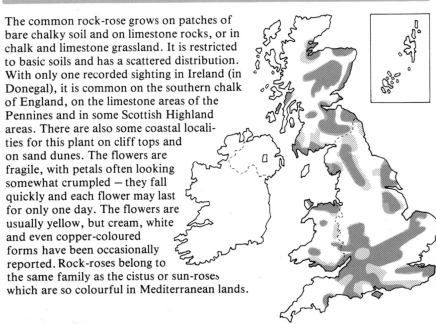

The common rock-rose grows on patches of bare chalky soil and on limestone rocks, or in chalk and limestone grassland. It is restricted to basic soils and has a scattered distribution. With only one recorded sighting in Ireland (in Donegal), it is common on the southern chalk of England, on the limestone areas of the Pennines and in some Scottish Highland areas. There are also some coastal localities for this plant on cliff tops and on sand dunes. The flowers are fragile, with petals often looking somewhat crumpled – they fall quickly and each flower may last for only one day. The flowers are usually yellow, but cream, white and even copper-coloured forms have been occasionally reported. Rock-roses belong to the same family as the cistus or sun-roses which are so colourful in Mediterranean lands.

Spring Gentian

Gentiana verna

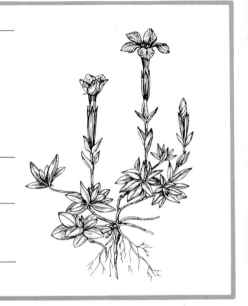

Size: 4/5 − 2½ in (2 − 6 cm).

Flowers: 1 1/5 − 1 4/5 in (3.0 − 4.5 cm) across; an intense brilliant blue, occasionally a clear paler blue. Petal tube 3/5 − 1 in (1.5 − 2.5 cm) long with 5 blunt, oval, spreading and flattened lobes and tiny upright lobelets between. Stigma white.

Leaves: basal leaves in a rosette, each leaf oval-pointed, 1/5 − 3/5 in (0.5 − 1.5 cm).

Growth: perennial plants with underground stems, and many tufted rosettes of leaves forming cushions in turf.

Flowering time: April − June.

Rare in Britain, spring gentian grows only in a few grassy or stony places on limestone in northern England, sometimes along riversides and by streams. In the west of Ireland, it grows on coastal limestone in turf and on rock ledges. At home in high mountain pastures across the world, this small gentian is one of a group of plants in the British Isles which may have survived or recolonised after the retreating ice of the last ice age. Since 1900, numbers have decreased; in some outlying localities flowers are sparse and the plants are declining in vigour − in some sites it is now extinct. Most spring gentian colonies in Britain are now in National Nature Reserves, to be treasured for the pleasure of seeing the unbelievable blue flowers scattered in the grass like sapphire stars.

Lady's-Slipper

Cypripedium calceolus

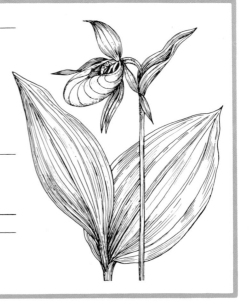

Size: 8 – 18 in (20 – 45 cm).

Flowers: 1 or 2 each stem; each with 4 narrow, spreading, maroon-coloured sepals, 2 1/2 – 3 1/2 in (6 – 9 cm), often slightly twisted on older flowers. The large hollow, yellow lip is the 'slipper' of the name; inside the lip is more or less spotted with red.

Leaves: 3 or 4 oval, pointed, clear green and strongly ribbed; partly sheathing the stem.

Growth: erect when in flower.

Flowering time: June – July.

This largest and most handsome of our British wild orchids has suffered so severely from the depredations of gardeners and botanists in the past that now we have one single record of a native plant growing in the wild. In Britain it has only grown in a few woods on limestone, so it has not ever been widespread. The attraction of its curious flowers proved irresistible in the days when the bounty of nature was thought to be limitless, and there was no awareness for the need for conservation of our natural treasures. Seed from the remaining flowers has not been successfully germinated for some years — possibly they are no longer fertile. Even though the lady's-slipper is now protected by law, it may be too late to save it for Britain.

The Lady's-slipper orchid is now known in only one remaining place in Britain as a British Wild Plant. To safeguard this solitary site the position has not been given.

Horseshoe Vetch

Hippocrepis comosa

Size: spreading to 16 in (40cm).

Flowers: heads of 5 – 12 flowers, radiating from top of stem in flattened, almost circular row. Each yellow flower small, up to 2/5 in (1 cm).

Fruit: characteristic curved pods, up to 1 1/5in (3 cm) long, with horseshoe-shaped segments.

Leaves: each 1 1/5 – 2 in (3 – 5 cm) with usually 3 – 8 pairs of leaflets along leaf stalk and 1 terminal leaflet.

Growth: nearly hairless, prostrate plant; flowerheads on long slender, curved stalks.

Flowering time: May – July.

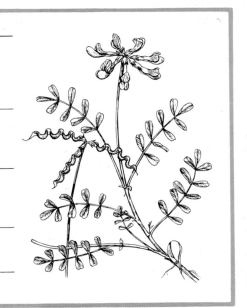

This is a local plant, not widespread, which grows only in dry calcareous grasslands and on cliffs, and is a soil indicator for chalk and limestone. It is found throughout southern Europe, with northern England as its northern limit. In England, the centre of distribution is the southern chalk; there are also scattered localities in Yorkshire, Lancashire, Cumbria and a local stronghold in Lincolnshire. A welcome sight with its neat bright clusters of miniature 'pea flowers', the fruits are also conspicuous; when ripe, the 'horseshoes' may be outlined by narrow bands of red-brown velvety papillae. Unable to compete with long, rough grass, the horseshoe vetch is less common on downland pastures now that fewer sheep graze there to give the famed close-cropped downland turf — the ideal habitat for many small flowers.

Bee Orchid

Ophrys apifera

Size: 6 – 24 in (15 – 60 cm).

Flowers: spike up to 5 in (12 cm) with usually 2 – 6 rather large flowers, distantly spaced on stem. Each flower 4/5 – 1 1/5 in (2 – 3 cm), with pink sepals, veined green, narrow green petals, and a large lip marked very distinctively to resemble a brown bumble bee visiting the flower.

Leaves: up to 3 in (8 cm), narrow oblong, rather blunt at tip, all unspotted.

Growth: hairless and shiny; leaves decreasing in size up the stem, grading into leaf-like bracts below each flower.

Flowering time: June – July.

All orchids have a special fascination — none more so than the 'insect mimics' with their curiously marked flowers, such as the bee orchid. Although seldom growing in quantity, it can be found in pastures and woodland on chalk and limestone, on base-rich clays and on calcareous coastal dunes. It occurs in England mainly in the south, Wales and, sparingly, in Northern Ireland. All orchids are unpredictable in growth and appearance from year to year, and it is a red-letter day when a flowering spike of a bee orchid is found unexpectedly on a downland slope. Orchids are very slow-growing — it may take 7 – 10 years for a bee orchid seedling to flower. So orchids should *never* be picked; if the flower is taken there will be no seed from that ten years' growth for the next generation.

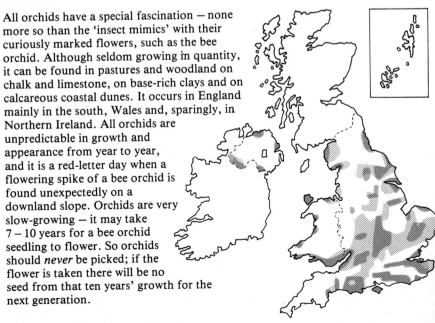

Musk Thistle

Carduus nutans

Size: 8 – 40 in (20 – 100 cm).

Flowers: flowerhead usually solitary, nodding, 1 1/5 – 2 in (3 – 5 cm), surrounded by spiny, often purplish bracts, star-shaped in bud.

Fruit: many small nut-like achenes, 1/4 in (6 mm) each with long whitish plume enabling seeds to be airborne and wind-dispersed.

Leaves: spear-shaped and deeply cut into lobes.

Growth: stiff, prickly; grey-white with cottony hairs; stems with spiny wing but smooth just below flowerheads.

Flowering time: May – August.

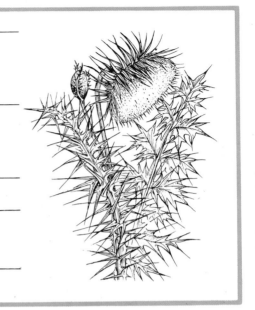

This thistle grows in pastures on calcareous soils, along roadsides, on bare chalk and in open scrub where not too shaded. It is locally common throughout England although less common in the north, and is absent from Ireland. It is recorded only very locally in Scotland and is never common there. Since 1930 Scottish sites have further decreased, leaving only 14 10-kilometre records; it is now all but extinct in Cumbria as well. Some thistles are agricultural weeds, pests to farmers – the creeping thistle (*Cirsium arvense)* is one of the four weeds legally controlled. The musk thistle, however, is an attractive plant with an interesting geometric design which is often a feature of the landscape – especially the long spines, star-shaped buds and the soft red-purple 'shaving brush' flowerheads.

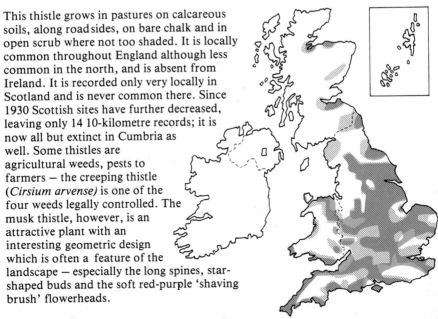

Round-leaved Sundew

Drosera rotundifolia

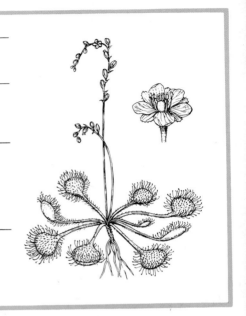

Size: 2½ – 10 in (6 – 25 cm).

Flowers: spike of shortly-stalked small flowers, 1/5 in (5 mm), with white petals.

Leaves: round reddish leaves up to 2/5 in (1 cm), on long red stalks, glistening with sticky glands.

Growth: leaves spread horizontally along the ground to form a basal rosette; slender reddish flower stems from centre, up to 10 in (25 cm) long.

Flowering time: June – August, but flowers inconspicuous; this plant can be recognised through the year by its leaves.

The round-leaved sundew grows on peat in bogs and in wet places on acid heaths and moors. It is often found growing in sphagnum mosses, and occasionally floating along the edges of small pools. A plant of the north and west, although decreasing through loss of suitable habitats, it is still widespread in Scotland, Wales and western Ireland, but only scattered in a few areas (such as the New Forest) in England. This striking plant is insectivorous, ie., it can capture and digest small creatures. The long, stalked, glandular hairs on the leaves are flexible — an insect landing on a leaf is soon trapped as the sticky hairs curve inwards. Digestive juices from the glands then kill and digest, providing useful minerals and proteins which are reabsorbed by the plant.

Yellow Saxifrage

Saxifraga aizoides

Size: 2 – 8 in (5 – 20 cm).

Flowers: 1 – 10 in a loose terminal inflorescence; 5 spreading triangular green sepals below showing between 5 narrow yellow petals which may be spotted red.

Leaves: many, 2/5 – 4/5 in (1 – 2 cm) long, rather thick and fleshy hairless leaves, densely covering the non-flowering shoots but spacing out towards flowerheads on flower stems.

Growth: many low-growing, leafy, non-flowering shoots and taller flowering stems.

Flowering time: April – July.

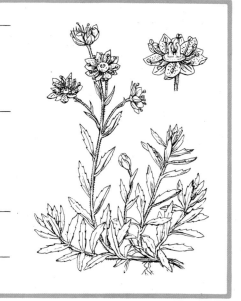

Yellow saxifrage is a plant of wet places, often growing in running water by streams and on wet stony ground in mountains. In Britain it is mainly restricted to Scotland where it can be found growing to nearly 4000 ft (1200 m), but it is absent from eastern Scotland. It grows on many of the Scottish islands, but not the Outer Hebrides. There are localities in Cumbria and a few along the west coast of Ireland. This is a plant of wild mountain scenery, and is an Arctic species, also growing in Arctic regions of Europe, Asia and North America. It is common on the mica-schist of the central Highlands in Scotland, sometimes against black shining wet rock — a striking background for the mass of yellow flowers and bright green leaves.

Heather

Calluna vulgaris

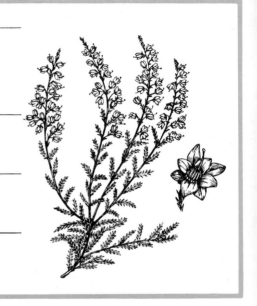

Size: to 2 ft (60 cm).

Flowers: many small ones in leafy, stalked spikes; 4 pale pink petals with 4 outer petal-like sepals. Occasionally white seen; said to bring good luck to finder.

Leaves: dark green; minute, closely overlapping along stems. Margins strongly inrolled making leaves 3-sided.

Growth: small evergreen shrub with tough, woody, sometimes twisting stems; plants may be downy.

Flowering time: July – October.

A delight of the countryside is a rolling expanse of purple heather moor. Heather (also known as 'ling') is a classic example of a plant which cannot tolerate lime in the soil, and is found therefore only on acid soils. It grows on moorlands, heaths and peat bogs, mainly in the north and west. Some heather moors are managed for grouse which feed off the young shoots; here, old straggly plants are regularly burned under controlled management to encourage the growth of young heather plants. When the need for timber was urgent, many acres of northern moorland and East Anglian heath were ploughed for forestry plantations and, with new afforestation techniques, more acres are ploughed each year. However, many acres of heather remain — some in National Parks — safe, we hope, for future years.

Bell Heather

Erica cinerea

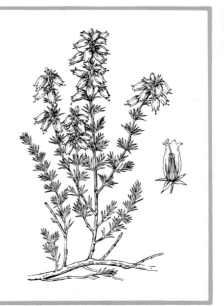

Size: to 2 ft (60 cm).

Flowers: in short spikes on the upper side-shoots. Each flower has 4 purple keeled sepals; petals crimson-purple and bell-shaped, the bell nearly globular and contracted at mouth, enclosing stamens and style.

Leaves: small, 1/5 in (6 mm); in whorls of 3; linear, hairless and dark green, with strongly inrolled margins.

Growth: small evergreen shrublets with many branched stems, rooting at base, with many bunched leafy shoots.

Flowering time: July – September.

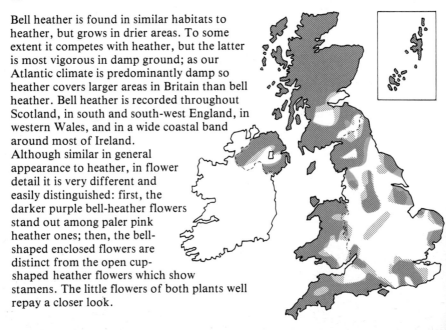

Bell heather is found in similar habitats to heather, but grows in drier areas. To some extent it competes with heather, but the latter is most vigorous in damp ground; as our Atlantic climate is predominantly damp so heather covers larger areas in Britain than bell heather. Bell heather is recorded throughout Scotland, in south and south-west England, in western Wales, and in a wide coastal band around most of Ireland.

Although similar in general appearance to heather, in flower detail it is very different and easily distinguished: first, the darker purple bell-heather flowers stand out among paler pink heather ones; then, the bell-shaped enclosed flowers are distinct from the open cup-shaped heather flowers which show stamens. The little flowers of both plants well repay a closer look.

Grass-of-Parnassus

Parnassia palustris

Size: 4 – 12 in (10 – 30 cm).

Flowers: single open flowers, 4/5 – 1 1/5 in (2 – 3 cm). 5 white petals which are clearly green-veined. 5 yellow stamens and 5 staminodes with many shining yellowish nectaries surrounding ovary.

Leaves: basal leaves 2/5 – 2 in (1 – 5 cm) long, pointed oval and deeply heart-shaped at base, with smooth margins.

Growth: hairless; the erect flower stem has single stalkless, heart-shaped leaf near base.

Flowering time: July – October.

This plant of marshes and wet moors is widespread in the north and west, but in rather scattered localities. In England it has decreased rapidly, and in Britain as a whole has become extinct in many counties — from the Isle of Wight in the south to Berwick in the north — in this century. In 1930 recorded extinctions included over 80 in England, several in Wales and nearly 50 in Ireland. This attractive plant with delicately veined, honey-scented white flowers suffers through loss of habitat as damp marshland is drained, but can still be found in upland pastures and on damp moorland. In Lancashire, Cheshire and Northern Ireland, the grass-of-parnassus grows in dune-slacks and is a distinct form with shorter, more compact growth and larger flowers.

Alpine Lady's-mantle

Alchemilla alpina

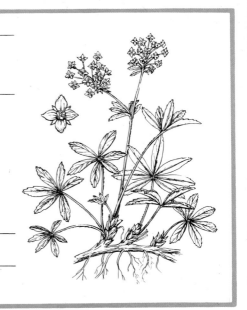

Size: 4 – 8 in (10 – 20 cm).

Flowers: many minute pale green flowers clustered in a branched inflorescence. No petals; 4 sepals and 4 stamens.

Leaves: basal leaves long-stalked, nearly circular in outline, 1 – 1 2/5 in (2.5 – 3.5 cm) across, each divided to base into 5 – 7 narrow segments. Upper surfaces green and hairless, lower surfaces densely silvery-silky, each segment often outlined with a row of silvery hairs.

Growth: creeping from rather woody stock.

Flowering time: June – August.

This plant of mountain grassland is widespread and locally abundant, but only in north-west Scotland, on the western islands and in Cumbria. It grows on screes, in rock crevices and on mountain tops; it has been recorded from 4000 ft (1200 m) in the Cairngorms, on the summits of Yorkshire peaks and at near sea-level on the Island of Skye. In some localities it can grow as the dominant plant, forming in some places a mountain-top '*Alchemilla*-lawn'. Related plants of this family are grown in gardens; all have the inconspicuous small greenish flowers, but also the distinctively-shaped leaves which hold the dew (an old Highland name for it was 'dew-cup'). The name 'lady's-mantle' comes from the attractive leaves, and '*Alchemilla*' from olden times when it was thought to be a powerful magic-working plant.

Snowdon Lily

Lloydia serotina

Size: 2 – 6 in (5 – 15 cm).

Flowers: single flower on slender stem, bell-shaped, opening in sunlight. Sepals and petals indistinguishable, appearing as 6 white petals, 2/5 in (1 cm), with brownish-red veins and yellowish centre.

Leaves: several thread-like leaves, 6 – 10 in (15 – 25 cm) long, and a few short, slightly wider stem leaves.

Growth: from a small bulb; plant hairless.

Flowering time: June.

This plant is very rare in Britain and grows only in Wales in the Snowdon range of mountains. Although so restricted for us, it is, however, widespread in distribution throughout the mountain regions of the Northern Hemisphere: from the Alps to the Urals, in Arctic Russia and Soviet Asia, in North America, China, Japan and the Himalayas. It is a plant of rock ledges on basic rock, and can be found growing in some of the world's grandest scenery. First recorded in Britain by David Lhwyd (for whom the plant is named) in about 1690, this scarce plant has become more rare through the depredations of plant collectors. Recorded on twelve cliffs in the recent past, it is today found on only five, and is now protected by law.

In Britain the Snowdon lily now grows in only one small area in the Snowdon range. To safeguard this solitary site the position has not been given. The photograph was taken in Switzerland.

Foxglove

Digitalis purpurea

Size: 20 – 60 in (50 – 150 cm).

Flowers: 20 – 80 stalked flowers in a long spike, each with a narrow bract. Sepals narrowly oval, sharply pointed at tips. Petal tube about 2 in (5 cm) long; pinkish-purple outside and inside distinctively marked with dark purple spots on white.

Fruit: oval capsule with long persistent style.

Leaves: 6 – 12 in (15 – 30 cm), oval or spear-shaped, the base narrowing to winged leaf-stalk.

Growth: biennial, with winter leaf rosettes.

Flowering time: June – September.

Foxgloves in woodland clearings, on heaths or on rocky mountains often grow in large numbers and are then a distinctive feature of these landscapes. They are widespread throughout Britain, except for central-eastern England, and are not common in central Ireland. This is a plant of light, dry acid soils, and it may be particularly dominant after fires. The foxglove was used for centuries as a country medicine as a cure for dropsy — long before the physician William Withering, in 1785, carried out tests on the plant to show that it contained a powerful heart medicine. The active constituents are still used today in controlled dosages in cardiac medicine. The finger-fitting shape of the flowers is reflected in many old country names for it: 'fingers and thumbs', 'fairy's thimbles', 'fairy fingers'.

Sea-kale

Crambe maritima

Size: 16 – 24 in (40 – 60 cm).

Flowers: many in a closely-branched head; each flower 2/5 – 3/5 in (1.0 – 1.5 cm) across; 4 white, rounded green-veined petals.

Fruit: green globular pods, to 3/5 in (1.5 cm) across.

Leaves: large, up to 1 ft (30 cm); fleshy with long thick stalks and leaf with crinkled, rounded, irregularly-toothed margins.

Growth: from fleshy rootstock; hairless, greyish-green or sometimes purple-tinged, stout and branched.

Flowering time: June – August.

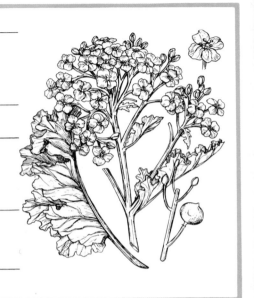

This seaside plant grows in some quantity in rather few places along our coastline. It can grow on sand, rocks and cliffs and, in some areas, on shingle banks. The thick fleshy plants are well adapted to withstand salt spray and even the occasional immersion by the sea. Formerly the sea-kale leaves were eaten, when vegetables were not available in the variety and continuity of supply that we have now: it became extinct from areas on the south-west coast from where it was collected for Covent Garden market. It would be sad to lose this handsome plant with its leaves and stems shot in pastel tones of grey, purple and green, and its attractive green 'bobble' fruits and strongly-scented flowers, whose scent, carried on the wind, is redolent of summer days by the sea.

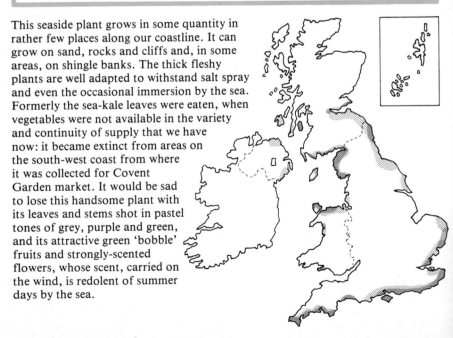

Common Sea-lavender

Limonium vulgare

Size: 3 – 12 in (8 – 30 cm).

Flowers: with papery bracts and flowers very closely spaced in 2 rows on upper side of angular branches of inflorescence, in short, dense, spreading spikes. Each flower, 3/10 in (8 mm), with funnel-shaped sepals and 5 broad, rounded, lilac or lavender petals.

Leaves: 2 – 6 in (5 – 15 cm), usually broadly spear-shaped but rather variable.

Growth: hairless, from branched woody stock; loose, tufted, carpeting rosettes of basal leaves.

Flowering time: July – October.

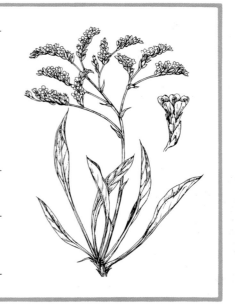

Common sea-lavender grows in muddy salt marshes but only in limited areas in Britain. Apart from a few localities in Wales, including Anglesey, it occurs in England but is restricted to several coastal areas, mainly around the Thames Estuary, Portsmouth Harbour, the Ribble Estuary and the Wash — all areas to some extent threatened by pollution and expanding industry. In a few localities, it carpets the mud-flats to the highwater line, covering large areas in tidal creeks and lagoons. When in flower it can be an expanse of lavender, partly covered by shallow seas with rising tides. Seven other sea-lavenders occur in Britain, all rather similar but distinguished by detail and some by differing requirements in type of coastal habitat; some of these are exceedingly rare with only one or two localities in Britain.

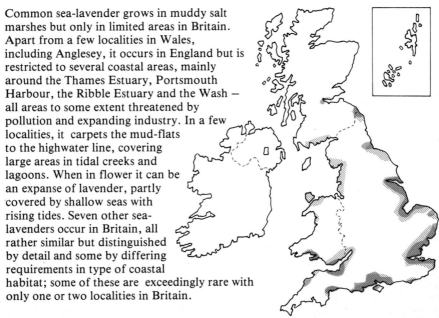

Sea Campion

Silene maritima

Size: 3 – 10 in (8 – 25 cm).

Flowers: 4/5 – 1 in (2.0 – 2.5 cm) across; 1 – 4 flowers in branched head with leafy bracts; each flower stalked; 5 white petals, each about 3/5 in (1.5 cm) wide, deeply cleft into 2 rounded, usually overlapping segments.

Fruit: broadly oval capsule with 6 recurved teeth.

Leaves: narrowly oval, rather stiff, fleshy and blue-green; narrowing up stems.

Growth: a loose cushion of prostrate non-flowering shoots from a branching woody stock.

Flowering time: June – August.

This plant grows mainly by the sea, but is also found, rather unexpectedly, as a plant of high mountains. It is familiar as a seaside plant as it grows on shingle, cliffs and on stony ground around almost the whole of Britain. Its few mountain sites, however, are very scattered, in Scotland, Wales, Cumbria and the Pennines; here it grows on rock-ledges, gravelly lakeshores and by alpine streams, at very nearly 4000 ft (1100 m). Most typically perhaps, sea campion is a plant of sea shingles, where the long branched roots and cushion formation play an important part in stablising the loose pebbles. Sometimes too it grows on unstable sand and here also contributes to fixing the dunes – this plant can withstand being temporarily covered by sand, pebbles and sea water.

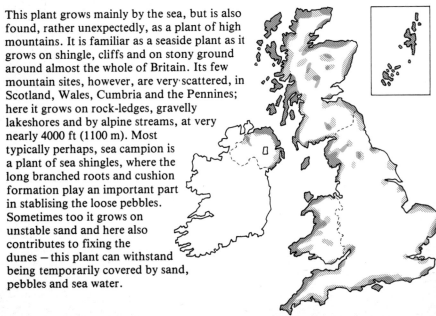

Thrift

Armeria maritima

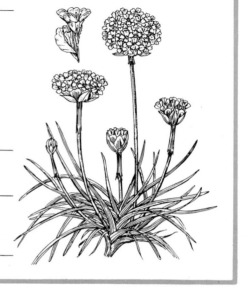

Size: 2 – 12 in (5 – 30 cm).

Flowers: in roundish heads, 3/4 – 1 in (1.5 – 2.5 cm) across, with a brown papery bract downwards on stem, and greenish sepals with bristle-teeth below flowerhead. Many flowers, 3/10 in (8 mm) across, tightly packed in head. Varying in colour from white through shades of pink.

Leaves: 4/5 – 6 in (2 – 15 cm), long, very narrow with one vein.

Growth: stout woody branched rootstock, rosettes of basal leaves; plant downy with short hairs.

Flowering time: April – October.

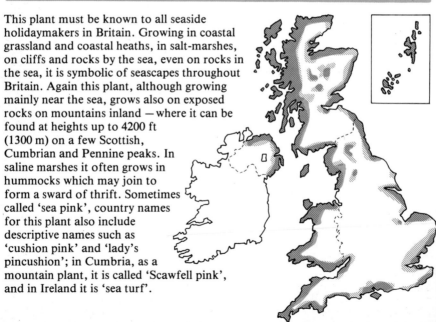

This plant must be known to all seaside holidaymakers in Britain. Growing in coastal grassland and coastal heaths, in salt-marshes, on cliffs and rocks by the sea, even on rocks in the sea, it is symbolic of seascapes throughout Britain. Again this plant, although growing mainly near the sea, grows also on exposed rocks on mountains inland — where it can be found at heights up to 4200 ft (1300 m) on a few Scottish, Cumbrian and Pennine peaks. In saline marshes it often grows in hummocks which may join to form a sward of thrift. Sometimes called 'sea pink', country names for this plant also include descriptive names such as 'cushion pink' and 'lady's pincushion'; in Cumbria, as a mountain plant, it is called 'Scawfell pink', and in Ireland it is 'sea turf'.

Burnet Rose

Rosa pimpinellifolia

Size: 6 – 20 in (15 – 50 cm).
Flowers: creamy white, 4/5 – 1 3/5 in (2 – 4 cm) across; each solitary on stalks usually with glandular bristles.
Fruit: almost globular, large hip, purplish-black when ripe, 2/5 – 3/5 in (1.0 – 1.5 cm), with persistent sepals.
Leaves: 3 – 5 pairs of small leaflets, 1/5 – 3/5 in (0.5 – 1.5 cm); each oval or almost circular with toothed margins, mostly hairless.
Growth: a low shrub, growing in large clumps through spread by suckers.
Flowering time: May – July.

Wild roses are a well-known feature of British landscapes — pink and white hedgerow roses in many varieties and many different species. To distinguish between them requires special study. One of the most distinctive is a low shrub, the burnet rose, which grows typically on sand dunes, also on sandy heaths and limestone pavement, mostly near the sea. This occurs mainly in the north and west of Britain, but also in scattered localities around almost the whole of our coastline, with some isolated records from inland areas of chalk and limestone. It was first recorded in Britain by John Gerard in his famous *Herbal* in 1597. One of our most beautiful wild flowers, its fiercely spiny stems contrast with the smooth petals which are creamy in bud and pure white in the golden-centred open flowers.

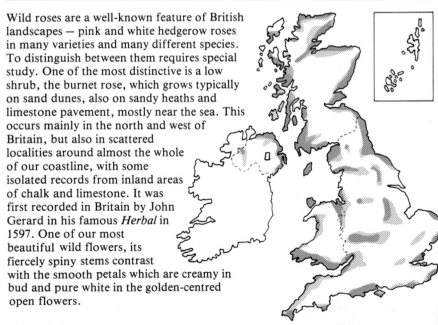

Viper's-bugloss

Echium vulgare

Size: 12 – 36 in (30 – 90 cm).

Flowers: in tall spikes of short branches with flowers and buds densely ranged along each branch. Each flower pink in bud, changing to vivid blue on opening. Petal tube 3/5 – 4/5 in (1.5 – 2.0 cm) long.

Fruit: 4 roughly wrinkled, angular nutlets hidden by sharp-pointed sepal-teeth.

Leaves: long, stalked, lower leaves up to 6 in (15 cm), with prominent mid-rib but no visible side-veins.

Growth: stems spotted and whole plant with bristly hairs.

Flowering time: June – September.

Viper's-bugloss grows on light, dry soils in grassy places by the sea, on sea cliffs, shingles and sand dunes. Here the vivid blue flower spikes are often spectacular when massed against the changing blues of the sea. It is also found rather frequently as a plant of waysides and waste places on well-drained soils in southern Britain. Rare in Scotland and Ireland, viper's-bugloss has scattered localities through central England, Wales and the west, but is most common in East Anglia and south-eastern England. The reference to the 'viper' in its name is of very early origin and refers to the nutlets, thought to resemble a viper's head in appearance. The changing colours in the flowers from pink to blue is characteristic of many of the plants in this family – the borage family.

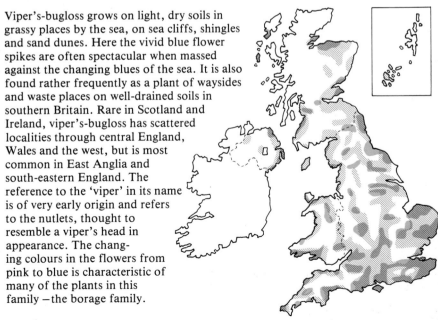

Yellow Horned-poppy

Glaucium flavum

Size: 12 – 36 in (30 – 90 cm).

Flowers: large yellow flowers, 2 2/5 – 4 in (6 – 10 cm) across, on short stalks; sepals with few long hairs, conspicuous on buds but soon falling as flower opens.

Fruit: very long thin curved capsule, 6 – 12 in (15 – 30 cm), is hairless but roughly wrinkled.

Leaves: lower leaves stalked, deeply divided into segments in different planes; upper leaves lobed and clasping the stem; all leaves rough.

Growth: shrubby with branched stem growing from deep, stout taproot.

Flowering time: June – September.

This plant grows mainly on the southern coasts of Britain; rare in Ireland, it grows as far north as Argyll on the west coast of Scotland. Although on the Continent it also grows in waste places inland, in Britain it is a maritime plant only. It is decreasing and is now almost extinct on our north-east coasts, and has gone from the Shetland Islands. In Britain it grows typically on shingle banks, where the deep roots are also well adapted to absorb the little moisture available below the dry surface pebbles. Known as a *'horned'* poppy from the long, curved pods of the fruit, it also has soft-petalled flowers like most poppies, which seem incredibly fragile in these rough, windswept habitats by the sea.

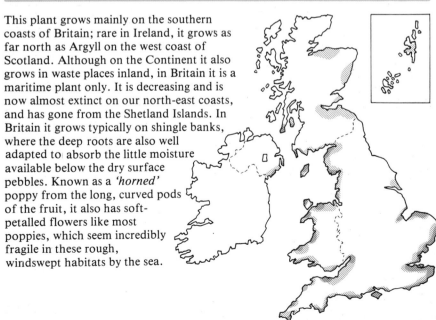

Wild Flowers and the Future

Plants are of vital importance to all animals—including man—and in many ways all of life is interdependent. On the island of Mauritius, almost 300 years ago in 1681, the dodo became extinct, possibly the best known of all extinctions—'dead as a dodo' is still an expression in common use. Recently it was discovered that one of the forest trees native to Mauritius, the *Calvaria major*, was dying out, with only 13 known specimens left on the island. On investigation it was noted that, although the trees produced fertile seed each year, the seeds are encased in an exceptionally thick, tough, woody shell and none have germinated for many years. Remnants of these seeds have been found in the skeletal remains of the dodo and it is now thought that only this bird had a beak of a sufficient size and strength to crack open the seeds and enable germination to proceed. Thus the tree was also doomed.

In recent times in Britain, we have similarly seen a sudden decrease in numbers of mute swans as the eelgrass (*Zostera marina*), on which the swans feed in muddy estuaries along our coast, was attacked by a plant disease and virtually disappeared. Fortunately in this case the eelgrass has recovered and the swans subsequently increased in numbers, dramatically demonstrating their interdependence.

Unlike today, wild flowers were, in the past, part of daily life. Starch from the tubers of lords-and-ladies was used in the laundry particularly to starch Elizabethan ruffs. Once primroses grew on Primrose Hill in London—now each year we must travel further from the city centres to find primroses. When old pastures were left to lie fallow, fields and downland carpeted with golden cowslips were part of the countryside in spring. Chequered fritillaries with the morning light shining through the flowers could be found growing by the thousands in damp meadows.

One of the possible ways to save endangered plants which is sometimes suggested is 'why not move the wild flowers from sites which are scheduled for destruction, and grow them elsewhere?' In fact it is not as easy as it would seem to grow wild plants—most have very specific habitat requirements, including soil, climate, aspect, associated plants and sometimes other factors. Often wild flowers will *not* grow in selected alternative sites, even when these appear to us to be exactly the same as the original natural habitat. It is therefore of vital importance to safeguard a range of natural habitats to save for the future as many as possible of Britain's wild flowers.

The statistics speak for themselves: it has been estimated that four per cent of the natural habitats in this country are destroyed annually. Ten species of British wild flowers became extinct in the past 100 years, and today 18 per cent of our native flora is to some extent threatened.

Our wild flowers are in danger. In Britain there are now enormous pressures on the land, with insufficient land to meet all the requirements of modern industry, increasing populations, new highways, increased-productivity farming regimes and so on. What can we do to help? We must think seriously about priorities. When threatened habitats are unique and irreplaceable, we should be prepared to stand by the choice of less financial gain where the alternative would be loss of a priceless part of our national heritage. Less nationally important sites may be lost as times must change, but we must take a stand and save our top-grade sites before it is too late. Individually we can help by spreading awareness of the need for conservation, and for practical action everyone interested in the countryside should join their local County Trust for Nature Conservation.

A Code of Conduct for the Conservation of Wild Plants

In the interests of conservation of the wild plants of this country, the Botanical Society of the British Isles has produced the following code:

Observe the law

Do not dig up wild plants without permission. It is now illegal for anyone, without permission of the owner or occupier, to dig up any wild plant.

Do not dig up or pick any protected plant. A small number of very rare plants in danger of extinction are totally protected by law (Conservation of Wild Creatures and Wild Plants Act, 1975) and removal of *any* part of these plants is an offence. The plants are:

Alpine Gentian *(Gentiana nivalis)*
Alpine Sow-thistle *(Cicerbita alpina)*
Alpine Woodsia *(Woodsia alpina)*
Blue Heath *(Phyllodoce caerulea)*
Cheddar Pink *(Dianthus gratianopolitanus)*
Diapensia *(Diapensia lapponica)*
Drooping Saxifrage *(Saxifraga cernua)*
Ghost Orchid *(Epipogium aphyllum)*
Killarney Fern *(Trichomanes speciosum)*
Lady's-slipper *(Cypripedium calceolus)*
Mezereon *(Daphne mezereum)*
Military Orchid *(Orchis militaris)*
Monkey Orchid *(Orchis simia)*
Oblong Woodsia *(Woodsia ilvensis)*
Red Helleborine *(Cephalanthera rubra)*
Snowdon Lily *(Lloydia serotina)*
Spiked Speedwell *(Veronica spicata)*
Spring Gentian *(Gentiana verna)*
Teesdale Sandwort *(Minuartia stricta)*
Tufted Saxifrage *(Saxifraga cespitosa)*
Wild Gladiolus *(Gladiolus illyricus)*

If you wish to identify a plant, take the smallest adequate bit. Often a sketch or photograph may serve the purpose. If living plants are needed for cultivation, take seed or cuttings sparingly and never from rare or protected plants.

Safeguard the habitat

For the conservation of our wild plants, the first essential is to preserve the sort of place and conditions they can grow in. They can easily and unwittingly be damaged by people. Watch your step. Treading compacts the soil, preventing seeding establishment and breaking off young shoots.

When you visit a rare plant, avoid doing anything which would expose it to unwelcome attention, such as making an obvious path to it or trampling on the vegetation around it.

'Gardening' before taking photographs may also give away the site. Bear in mind too how readily nearby plants can be crushed by the toes of kneeling photographers. Remember that photographs themselves can give clues to the localities of rare plants, quite apart from the information accompanying them.

Avoid telling people about the site of a plant you believe to be rare. Your local Nature Conservation Trust should, however, be informed. They will help safeguard it.

Respect requests from conservation bodies or landowners not to visit particular sites at certain times.

No specimens should be taken from any nature reserve, nature trail or National Trust property.

Teachers and leaders of outings and field meetings are particularly urged to bear these points in mind.

Avoid thoughtless introductions

Plants should not be introduced into the countryside without the knowledge and agreement of your local Nature Conservation Trust, or of the Botanical Society of the British Isles. (See 'Societies and Nature Reserves' for their addresses.)

National Nature Reserves

The Nature Conservancy Council has established 159 National Nature Reserves; some are owned or leased by the Council, others are established under a nature reserve agreement with the owners. Information on any of these or about the Council itself can be obtained from its Great Britain Headquarters: Nature Conservancy Council, 20 Belgrave Square, London SW1X 8PY. N.B: All the reserves have different regulations and many require permits before entry. Get in touch with the regional offices before trying to enter them.

The following is a listing of all the 159 Reserves, region by region, with the address of the regional office of the Council, and the names of the Reserves followed by the number which keys it to the map.

England: South-west Region
Roughmoor, Bishops Hull, Taunton, Somerset TA1 5AA.

Arne (134); Avon Gorge (115); Axmouth-Lyme Regis Undercliffs (141); Bovey Valley Woodlands (137); Braunton Burrows (129); Bridgwater Bay (125); Dendles Wood (139); Ebbor Gorge (124); Hartland Moor (140); Morden Bog (133); Rodney Stoke (123); Shapwick Heath (126); Studland Heath (135); Yarner Wood (138).

England: South-east Region
'Zealds', Church Street, Wye, Ashford, Kent TN25 5BW.

Castle Hill (142); Ham Street Woods (128); Blean Woods (121); High Halstow (118); Kingley Vale (131); Lullington Heath (132); Stodmarsh (122); The Swale (143); Swanscombe Skull Site (119); Tring Reservoirs (104); Wye and Crundale Downs (127).

England: West Midland Region
Attingham Park, Shrewsbury, Salop SY4 4TW.

Chaddesley Woods (92); Chartley Moss (76); Derbyshire Dales (61); Rostherne Mere (56); Workman's Wood (144); Wren's Nest (85); Wybunbury Moss (65); Wyre Forest (145).

England: East Midland Region
P.O. Box 6, Godwin House, George Street, Huntingdon, Cambs PE18 6BU.

Castor Hanglands (83); Chippenham Fen (93); Holme Fen (86); Knocking Hoe (105); Monks Wood (89); Saltfleetby-Theddlethorpe Dunes (55); Woodwalton Fen (90).

England: East Anglia Region
60 Bracondale, Norwich, Norfolk NOR 58B.

Bure Marshes (81); Cavenham Heath (94); Hales Wood (106); Hickling Broad (80); Holkham (67); Leigh (117); Orfordness-Havergate (107); Scolt Head Island (66); Swanton Novers Woods (72); Thetford Heath (91); Walberswick (95); Weeting Heath (87); Westleton Heath (96); Winterton Dunes (77).

England: North-west Region
Blackwell, Bowness-on-Windermere, Windermere, Cumbria LA23 3JR.

Ainsdale Sand Dunes (54); Asbyscar (146); Blelham Bog (48); Clawthorpe Fell (147); Gait Burrows (148); Glasson Moss (45); Moor House (46); North Fen (49); Roudsea Wood (51); Rusland Moss (50).

England: North-east Region
33 Eskdale Terrace, Newcastle-upon-Tyne NE2 4DN.

Coom Rigg Moss (42); Lindisfarne (38); Long Gill (52); Upper Teesdale (47).

Scotland: South-west Region
The Castle, Loch Lomond Park, Balloch, Dunbartonshire.

Ben Lui (31); Caerlaverock (44); Cairnsmore of Fleet (149); Glasdrum Wood (29); Glen Diomhan (37); Kirkconnell Flow (43); Loch Lomond (36); Silver Flowe (41); Taynish (150); Tynron Juniper Wood (40).

Scotland: South-east Region
12 Hope Terrace, Edinburgh EH9 2AS.

Ben Lawers (151); Caenlochan (25); Isle of May (35); Loch Leven (34); Meall Nan Tarmachan (30); Morton Lochs (33); Rannoch Moor (28); Tentsmuir Point (32); Whitlaw Mosses (39).

Scotland: North-west Region
Fraser Darling House, 9 Culduthel Road, Inverness IV2 2 AG.

Allt Nan Carnan (17); Ariundle Oakwood (152); Beinn Eighe (16); Coile Thocabhaig (153); Corrieshalloch (13); Glen Roy (24); Gualin (7); Inchnadamph (9); Invernaver (6);

Inverpolly (10); Loch Druidibeg (18); Loch Maree Islands (159); Monach Isles (14); Mound Alderwoods (12); Nigg and Udale Bays (158); North Rona and Sula Sgeir (3,4); Rassal Ashwood (15); Rhum (21); St Kilda (11); Strathy Bog (8); Strathfarrar (153).

Scotland: North-east Region

Wyne-Edwards House, 17 Rubislaw Terrace, Aberdeen AB1 1XE.

Cairngorms (22); Craigellachie (20); Dinnet Oakwood (23); Haaf Fruney (2); Hermaness (1); Keen of Hamar (154). Morrone Birkwoods (26); Muir of Dinnet (155); Noss (5); St Cyrus (27); Sands of Forvie (19).

Wales: North Wales Region

Penrhos Ffordd, Bangor, Gwynedd LL57 2LQ.

Cader Idris (82); Coed Aber (156); Coed Camlyn (71); Coed Cymerau (69); Coed Dolgarrog (60); Coed Ganllwyd (79); Coed Gorswen (59); Coed Y Rhygen (74); Coed Tremadoc (70); Coedydd Maentwrog (68); Cors Erddreiniog (57); Cwm Glas Crafnant (63); Cwm Idwal (62); Morfa Dyffryn (78); Morfa Harlech (73); Newborough Warren/Ynys Llanddwyn (58); Rhiong (75); Y Wyddfa-Snowdon (64).

Wales: Dyfed-Powys Region

Plas Gogerddan, Aberystwyth, Dyfed SY23 3 EB.

Allt Rhyd y Groes (99); Coed Rheidol (88); Cors Tregaron (97); Craig Cerrig Gleisiad (100); Craig y Cilau (101); Dyfi (84); Nant Irfon (98); Ogof Ffynnon Ddu (157); Skomer (111).

Wales: South Wales Region

44 The Parade, Roath, Cardiff CF2 3AB.

Cwm Clydach (102); Gower Coast (113); Oxwich (114); Whiteford (112).

National Nature Reserves

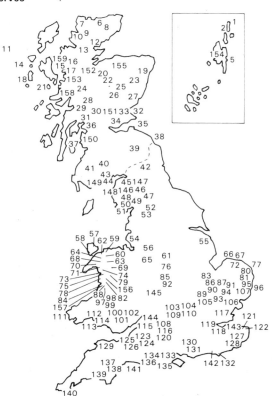

Glossary

Achene: small, dry, nutlike single-seeded fruit.

Anaerobic: able to survive in the absence of free oxygen.

Anther: part of the stamen containing the pollen grains.

Appressed: pressed closely against, but not joined to—e.g. hairs to a stem

Axil: angle between a bract (or leaf) and the stem on which it grows.

Biennial: plants which require two years to complete their life-cycle.

Blade: flat expanded portion of a leaf.

Calyx: outer part of a flower (i.e. the sepals) which protect the inner flower.

Calyx tube: formed by the fusion of individual sepals.

Capsule: dry fruit of two or more carpels which opens to release seeds.

Carpel: tiny folded modified leaf in the centre of the female flower. It may be separate or several fused together; after fertilisation it becomes the fruit.

Corolla: petals of a flower.

Crenate: having shallow rounded scalloped margins.

Crenulate: as crenate, but with smaller neater indentations.

Deltoid: triangular, like the Greek letter *delta*.

Dioecious: having male and female flowers on separate plants.

Dune-slacks: low-lying damp or wet areas among sand dunes.

Filament: stalk of an anther.

Flora: word capitalised: book describing the vegetation and individual plants of a particular area.

Floret: one complete flower in a flower spike, or in a composite flowerhead.

Gynoecium: female part of the flower, made up of one or more ovaries with their styles and stigmas.

Hermaphrodite: having both sexes in one flower.

Inflorescence: head of flowers; stalked inflorescences are of various patterns, e.g. spike or umbel.

Inrolled: edge of a leaf rolled in towards the centre.

Jizz: describing the intangible but recognisable overall characteristics of a living thing, such as a plant or bird.

Leach: where rain (carrying carbon dioxide) dissolves and washes out the calcium salts from the upper layers of the soil.

Leaf-margin: edge around the outer perimeter of a leaf.

Mid-rib: central vein of a leaf, often thickened and conspicuous.

Monoecious: having separate male and female flowers, with both on same plant (*cf* dioecious).

Nectaries: small glands which exude nectar, usually at the base of a flower and attracting pollinating insects.

Node: point on the stem where one or more leaves arise.

Ovary: hollow in a carpel in which the ovules (eggs), which develop into seeds after fertilisation, are enclosed.

Palmately: a palmate leaf is one with several lobes from a central point.

Papillae: small elongated projections.

Perennial: plant which lives for many years, mostly trees and shrubs; some herbaceous perennials grow again from the root each year.

Perianth: outer parts of a flower, normally sepals and petals.

Pinnate: a leaf with a single main leaf-stalk and a number of separate leaflets attached to it.

Relict: left behind, as with fragments of arctic vegetation from late glacial times still growing today in isolated pockets in upland Britain.

Revolute: rolled downwards.

Rhizome: horizontal underground stem which acts as a food store and as a means of vegetative reproduction.

Rootstock: overwintering roots of a perennial plant.

Sepals: outer perianth segments of the flower, usually green and leaf-like.

Spadix: thick fleshy flowering spike of *Arums* (and other lilies).

Spathe: large bract protecting a spadix, as in lords-and-ladies.

Spike: long narrow inflorescence of flowers which are attached directly to main stem without flower stalks.

Stamen: male part of the flower, consisting of filament (stalk) and pollen-producing anther.

Staminode: sterile, non pollen-producing stamen.

Stigma: surface of carpel receptive to pollen grains, often sticky or feathery.

Stipule: outgrowth of the base of a leaf-stalk, often leaf-like but sometimes modified to a spine.

Stolon: modified stem growing horizontally above the ground and rooting at the nodes.

Style: stalk joining carpel to stigma and holding up stigma prominently to catch pollinating insects or wind-borne pollen. Absent in some plants.

Taproot: main root growing straight down into the soil which anchors the plant firmly in the ground.

Taxonomy: science of classifying and naming living organisms; *plant taxonomist* is one who studies the classification and relationships of plants.

Terminal: borne at the end of a stem.

Trifoliate: leaves with three leaflets (as in wood sorrel).

Tuber: swollen portion of root or stem lasting one year only.

Umbel: radiating inflorescence of stalked flowers all arising from the same point, as in cow parsley, hemlock water-dropwort and other members of the *Umbelliferae.*

Umbellifer: member of the *Umbelliferae family.*

Whorl: circular group of leaves or flowers all leaving the stem at one level.

Index